TINMAN to IRONMAN

TINMAN to IRONMAN

26.2 Proven Ways to Crush Your Failures and Transform Your Life Today!

CHRIS SWANSON

NEXT CENTURY
PUBLISHING

Tinman to Ironman

Published by Next Century Publishing
www.NextCenturyPublishing.com

ISBN: 978-162-9038438

Printed in the United States of America

PROLOGUE

TIN:

Tin is a shiny metal that, on the outside, gives the world an impression of beauty and glamour. It glistens under the sun and makes for a bright surface. But once you get past the surface, that's where it all stops. The outside looks appealing, but under pressure, tin crumbles. It has no stability, no structure, and no long-term use. *Tin* can't hold up.

Folks all around you build their lives on a tin foundation. They look so put together, but give them a little adversity, and they quickly tap out. Families, businesses, and each one of us—when built on a tin foundation—fall apart when tragedy strikes or when temptation rears its ugly head. Tin has no place in the life of a champion. No place in the life of a game changer. If you have areas in your life that look good on the outside and yet you know you can't withstand an upcoming storm, fix them. Trade them. Strap on the metal of strength and build a foundation of IRON!

IRON:

Iron isn't shiny, pretty, or desirable. But it's tough. It can take the heat in more ways than one. *Tin* has a melting point of 449.5 degrees Fahrenheit, whereas iron doesn't melt until 2,800 degrees Fahrenheit! On the outside, iron might look dull and unattractive, but it's what the earth's core is made of.

Let me assure you, when the wheels of your life are falling off, you want an *iron* foundation. You want *iron* friends. You want an *iron* attitude. Iron stares down the barrel of pressure and refuses to blink. Being made of iron prepares you to change lives, including your own. If you want it, if you need it, then here is your plan to achieve it. For the first time in your life, take a stand! Promise yourself: this is the day that I begin to transform my life from a *Tinman* to an *IRONMAN*!

Your journey of hope begins now...

INTRODUCTION

I didn't grow up wealthy. I didn't do well in school, and I wasn't physically gifted. I was never popular. But I connected with almost everybody. I was a cute kid only in the opinion of my Grandma Ford and my mom. From childhood to adulthood, I look back now and see that I represent a society that is big in numbers. In fact, I'm part of the majority, the center of the bell curve, the population we work with, play with, and worship with every day. I am an "Average Joe" or, if I were a girl, an "Average Jane."

In 2007, something changed the perception I had of myself, an event that set in motion a lifetime of success. It was the morning after I had finished my first Ironman in Panama City, Florida. It wasn't because I had won anything. It was because the odds were stacked against me. I wasn't supposed to be the guy that could do an Ironman. The world had told me for thirty-five years that it was something I could not accomplish. I did it anyway.

Around 5:30 the morning after, I was unable to sleep, so I quietly slipped downstairs to the hotel lobby. I ordered a large, cold glass of orange juice. As I sipped my drink, I wrote three letters, one to each of my boys and one to my wife. In the letters, I wrote how thankful I was for their sacrifice and followed up with how much I loved them. The letters were filled with emotion and sealed with gratitude. When I finished, I just sat there alone, my medal still hanging around my neck, thinking about how it had all happened. Not just the Ironman, but my life. How had an average person gone from nothing to feeling like a champion? And if I could do it, why shouldn't I tell others what I did to get where I was so that they could do it for themselves?

Back at the hotel later that day, we packed to leave, and I noticed in more detail a banner my wife had made for me at the finish line. My family and friends had written messages on it for me. As I reread it, one of the messages on the top right corner stood out. In fact, it came to define my life. Written by one of the wisest men I have ever met— Jack Pichette, a Bible scholar and a friend for life—it read: *"Swanson—you are no longer a TINMAN. You are forever an IRONMAN!"*

My eyes filled with tears. He was right. What had happened to me could never be taken away. A feeling of euphoria swept over me; I vowed at that moment to take inventory of my life, pick out the areas where I had achieved victory, and teach other people how they could be an *Ironman* in their own lives. What if you could be the hero to your kids, pay off your debts, restore a relationship, and become a multi-millionaire? What if...? And that is how *Tinman to IRONMAN* was born.

You may never want to swim 2.4 miles, bike 112 miles, or run 26.2 miles, but what if you were able to beat whatever was keeping you down? What if you could overcome whatever it is that is destroying your dreams? Each one of us has an Ironman to complete. What's yours?

The next 26.2 chapters of application will show you just that. You will learn to stack victory upon victory.

IRONMAN is my story, told to inspire you to write your own story of how you've transformed your life from *Tinman to IRONMAN!*

TABLE OF CONTENTS

What Do You Get with a Crackhead, 200 Hot Tamales, and a Cop?

●●●

I was on patrol, the second shift, around six o'clock at night, driving northbound I-475, just inside the Flint city limits. The sky was a ghostly gray with a hint of bitter cold in the air. Ahead of me, my eyes fixed on an older model Chevy station wagon with beat-up, fake wood-paneled sides. It looked to me like there was only one occupant. The car hugged the inside lane and drifted back and forth in its lane.

I wasn't sure if he was drunk, so I pulled my fully marked police car up close behind him, hit my emergency lights, and made the stop. I called dispatch and relayed the license plate number and my location. As I approached, my eyes scanned the interior of the vehicle. I saw purses, fast food wrappers, and the disheveled carcass of a man behind the wheel. His hair was unkempt and his face gaunt. His clothes were layered in filth and odor.

"Sir, I need to see your driver's license, registration, and proof of insurance." He gave me the 1,000-mile stare. "Do you have a valid license?" I asked.

"No," he slowly replied.

"Sir, I need you to step out of the vehicle and place your hands behind your back." Without resistance, he stepped out and did as I said. I snapped the cuffs around his wrists and patted him down for weapons, then walked him back to my patrol car. Once he was secured in the backseat with the barrier between us, I sat down to run him through the Law Enforcement Information Network (LEIN) to see if he and the car were even legal. As I suspected, they weren't. The driver had a few misdemeanor warrants, his driving privileges were suspended, his beat-up station wagon wasn't registered, and he had no insurance. His stare continued every time I spoke to him. Remembering the purses in the car, I asked why he had them. His head fell down in shame. I waited for just a moment, until his lower chin started to quiver, and he confessed that he had stolen them. I sensed despair in his voice, so I looked directly at him through my rearview mirror and asked, "Bro, what's your story?

He cleared his throat and said, "I have been addicted to crack for years. I lost my wife and my family because of it. I have no job and I'm starving. I woke up in my car and felt so helpless and alone that I just started driving north from Detroit, not knowing what would happen or where I would end up. And that's when you pulled me over...I'm broken."

His voice sounded as innocent as a child speaking to his mother. His story was both convincing and humbling.

An overwhelming sense of compassion compelled me to change what I, or any other policeman for that matter, would normally have done in the situation. I called for a wrecker to impound his car. I finished my vehicle inventory and confirmed my suspicions that the purses had been stripped of all valuables, including their owners' information.

As I waited for the wrecker, I adjusted the rearview mirror and locked eyes with that man. He sat motionless. I told him, "Sir, there is something about you that is telling me you are different and in need of major help, maybe even a second chance. I could write you a bunch of tickets and take you to jail, but I'm not going to. Instead, I'm towing your car and taking you to a place where you can get the help you need. But it's only going to work if you want it to. Do you understand me?"

Judging by his stunned look, I surmised he'd had some bad run-ins with the police in the past and was totally unsure about what I was going to do. Regardless, he acknowledged with a nod. Looking back, it didn't matter what he thought. I already had a plan.

Once the car had been loaded on the tow truck and taken away, I traveled north to the Robert T Longway exit. I followed the Boulevard to Garland and then turned south at the corner of 5th Avenue, to the front doors of the Carriage Town Mission, a Christian-based homeless shelter I've known for years. I stepped out of my cruiser, walked to the right rear, and opened the back door. "Step out, please. I want you to know that if my sergeant ever found out what I was doing, I would be in huge trouble. But I'm giving you two choices: you can walk up those steps and get the help you need to save your life, or you can go back to the streets and die in a ditch. Do you understand me? I don't want to know what you chose; that's up to you."

He affirmed with a nod that he understood. I released him, got back into my police cruiser, and drove away. As I did, I could see him in the rearview mirror, standing in the street watching me fade away. I turned the corner and disappeared into the night.

To this day, I don't know his name or his life story.

Two years later...

Everybody in the patrol division must do their time at the corner of Pierson and Martin Luther King Boulevard. The heart of the ghetto. That's where the McCree Public Health clinic is located. It provides service to low- and no-income families. The police are there because it's not uncommon for the ugliness of violence to strike. People fight and cars get stolen if the police are not there. One spring afternoon, I was sitting in the north end of the lot when I noticed a group of volunteers about to toss boxes of something in the dumpster.

I climbed out of my vehicle and strode over to them. "What are you doing?" I asked.

"These are hot tamales that the Flint schools had left over from lunch and we can't keep them. The weekend is here and they'll go bad, so we have to throw them away."

I hate waste, so I convinced them to give the food to me, and I would drop it off at the Carriage Town Mission on my way back to the sheriff's office. They agreed and within 10 minutes, we had loaded 200 hot tamales on white Styrofoam trays, wrapped in cellophane, into my 1998 Chevy police cruiser. Once my shift ended, I left the lot and detoured to Carriage Town. I walked to the front door, rang the buzzer, and was greeted with a crackly, "May I help you?" I told them I was from the sheriff's office, and I had these tamales I wanted them to have. The voice responded with another crackly, "Sure, thanks so much. I'll send someone out to help you unload them."

Within minutes, three workers came out and grabbed a box each to take to the mess hall. Once inside, I thanked them for the help and began the walk back to my cruiser.

Just then, a soft voice came from behind. I turned to see one of the workers who had helped me unload the tamales. "Sir, you don't remember me, do you?" I didn't. The man continued, "Two years ago, you dropped me off at this mission, and I've never left. I just wanted to thank you for giving me a second chance." I stood there, stunned. There before me was the once disheveled crackhead from my traffic stop two years prior. He had chosen to live. He had chosen to serve the Lord and stay clean from his addiction. I shook his hand, gave him a hug, and told him how proud I was of him.

I left the mission with more than a smile. That day, a former crackhead had given me more than I could have ever given him: a lesson in belief that not everybody makes the best choices in life, but a second chance might be all it takes to change a life forever.

Each of us makes decisions every day. We choose to complain or compliment. We choose to give up or fight. We choose to live a life of purpose or die a death of cowardice. It all comes down to our choices. And when you make bad choices, sometimes all you need to get back on your feet is a second chance.

So, what do you get with a crackhead, 200 hot tamales, and a cop? One of the best illustrations of a second chance that saved a man's life.

Iron Theme:
- Believe in Second Chances.

Action Steps:
- Encourage those who are struggling, no matter how bleak their life might be.
- Never give up on others.
- Never give up on yourself.

MURDER BY CHOICE

● ● ●

Jennifer Martin came from a loving home. Although raised in a divorced family, her mother and father loved her. She lived in an affluent community and went to a Class "A" school. She was beautiful, loving mother with intelligence to boot. She had the potential of a rock star. But that would all change the day she chose to smoke her first marijuana joint. Her "boyfriend" invited her to try weed at a party. For whatever reason, she chose to do it. Unbeknownst to her, the joint was laced with cocaine, and she got more than a buzz. At that moment, the "dragon" entered her body—the dragon that would ultimately take her life. That night her choice led to decades of broken relationships, debt, prostitution, overdoses, and distrust. Jennifer Martin would regret that day for the next thirty years. She never grew up to be a doctor or a lawyer; she grew to become an addict.

July 23, 2010, an hour before noon. The day was rainy and cold, and the clouds were gray. Rain turned to snow. Within the city stood a two-bedroom, two-story apartment, building 19, apartment 6, with neighbors on both sides. Inside the front door, the staircase was situated to the right and the kitchen to the left. The body lay in the kitchen, on her back with her head near the hallway. It was the lifeless body of forty-six-year-old Jennifer Marie Martin, surrounded by pictures of her family and her decorations, a cross of Christ hanging on the wall above her microwave.

Earlier that morning, Jennifer's father, Charlie Gannon, came to pick her up for a scheduled rehab appointment. She had been clean for a good length of time and then fell off the wagon. But her daddy never gave up.

Fighting to the end, he offered help to his little girl to try and beat the dragon. When he knocked on her door that morning, there was no response. Using a spare key, he opened the door to what would be a nightmare that would never end. Charlie found his baby lying lifeless on the cold tile floor. He desperately called her name with no response. He saw that she wasn't breathing and called 911. In a panic, he tried to find a pulse and couldn't. Her pink bathrobe was wrapped tightly around her neck with the terry cloth belt knotted below her ears. He thought maybe she had hung herself and told that to the dispatcher. Charlie did everything a seventy-one-year-old man could do for his daughter.

Police and paramedics rushed to the scene and immediately knew something wasn't right. Their "Spidey senses" immediately kicked in. There was no way Jennifer could have hung herself. There was nothing in the middle of the kitchen area to tie off to, and it's impossible to choke yourself to death. So what happened to her? A cursory search found even more disturbing details. The phone cord had been ripped from the wall. The living room, just beyond the kitchen, had been torn apart, valuables had been taken, and her 1997 dark blue Chevy Silverado with a dent in the left rear quarter panel was stolen. Jennifer Martin had been robbed and murdered!

As the crime scene specialist arrived, the responding officers broadcasted a Be On (the) Look Out (BOLO) message over central dispatch for a the Silverado. At the time, it was believed that whoever was driving the truck was either the murderer or certainly held some very valuable information about the case. Without any other leads, her vehicle became the focus of the investigation.

As the Captain of Law Enforcement for the sheriff's office, I commanded more than seventy-five people. My divisions included patrol, courts, narcotics, the detective bureau, and crime scene investigations.

What made this case personal to me was that my crime scene investigator was Deputy Jack Gannon, the victim's baby brother. Jack and I graduated from high school together, we worked together, and we are still friends. I will never forget the moment the call was first dispatched. Jack and I were working on a project in my office. He heard the address and knew it was his sister's home. In my business, we take care of our own. If my partner's family is hurt, my family is hurt. If his or her family needs help, I help. Jack's sister had been murdered, and I dropped everything. I arranged for him to get to the scene and comfort his broken father. I dispatched every car I had available, marked and unmarked, with one goal in mind: we were going to find her Silverado with the dent on the left side, and we were going to track down those who were responsible.

That day, at approximately 12:56 p.m., I fell into one of the most interesting police experiences of my career.

Every car we had was on the street looking for the vehicle, and mine was no exception. I left my downtown office and randomly picked northbound Saginaw to travel on, which led to the north end of Flint. I had no hunch or clue, but my choice to drive this route paid off. I studied every vehicle I passed with intensity. I searched the parking lots and kept watch for abandoned vehicles.

Approximately six miles north of downtown, my eyes locked on a dark-colored truck heading south in the curb lane. I glanced quickly to my left as it passed by and there it was – the Silverado with a dent in the left rear. There appeared to be two subjects in the front seats. I spun my unmarked car around and rolled up on their rear. A bumper sticker to the left of the trailer hitch read, "My Child is a Dolen Middle School Honor Roll Student." The victim's daughter had earned that recognition. I threw my tactical vest over my head and grabbed my radio. I tried to key up the mic, but other officers had traffic, and I couldn't get in to call out the plate.

What was only seconds seemed like hours. By that time, the killers knew that the white boy driving the black Tahoe with tinted windows behind them must be a cop. The chase was on. Still unable to call the stop in, we picked up speed when they tried to lose me on the side streets. Not happening. Finally, there was a break in radio traffic, and I called in, "104," which was my call number.

Dispatch responded, "104 go ahead."

"I'm following a dark blue Silverado, plate number DTH 1990."

After a short pause, dispatch continued, "104, that's going to be the wanted vehicle in the Flint homicide; I need some cars to be with 104."

Like music to my ears, my brothers and sisters in uniform answered to back me up. By that time, the vehicle ahead of me was really trying to lose me, and we ended up stopped at a major intersection, Martin Luther King and Pasadena Avenue. There was no question the suspects were in a panic, and I was determined to leave them no time to make any decisions that would enable them to get away. I was staying on their bumper until backup arrived. The only problem was, no backup was arriving.

The suspect punched the vehicle through the intersection, then jerked the vehicle to the right into a BP gas station and stopped. I stayed right on their tail until both of us were parked. I knew they were asking themselves if they should run, shoot, or give up. For me, it was easy. They either listened to my orders, or I killed them.

No backup had shown up yet; they were on their way, but in that instance, if they were two minutes off, it might as well have been an hour. "104, we're at the BP station at MLK and Pasadena," I told dispatch. I got out of my vehicle and crossed over to the passenger side of the truck where I could see the two inside. The passenger door popped open. They must have known they could either go peacefully or be killed, and they chose to live another day. In those situations, police officers cannot show weakness or uncertainty in their voices; we need to command the scene.

The killers climbed out of the passenger door and obeyed my verbal commands to lie on their bellies, spread-eagled.

With them on the ground, I waited for only a minute until my first backup car arrived, Deputy Mo Sanchez. What a sight to see. He trained his pistol on the suspects while I transitioned and cuffed them one at a time. As more help arrived, we searched their clothes and found the victim's cell phone in the driver's coat pocket.

Martin's vehicle was loaded with stolen property from her home. These guys were clearly the suspects we had been searching for. They were taken to the detective bureau where they both confessed to the murder of Jennifer Martin earlier that morning. In fact, they were on their way to dump the truck at Devil's Lake prior to being stopped. Had they made it, the likelihood of ever solving the crime would have been minimal. Between a plea deal and a jury trial, her killers were sentenced to life in prison.

I will forever remember how that day unfolded and how personal the case was. More importantly, I felt honored to have played a role in bringing closure to this family. This was not a random crime; it was deliberate. The killers knew Jennifer Martin because they were her suppliers, and the robbery and murder were planned. The most revealing aspect of this entire tragedy is how Jennifer Martin's decision 30 years earlier was the catalyst that started this tragic tale of events. What if she never smoked that joint? Who knows what kind of future would she have had? Instead, her choices plunged her into a decline of events that led her astray and may have even contributed to her death.

We all have choices to make. We choose what to eat, what to wear, which college to attend, what to drive, and even whom we marry. Life is about choices. What we all need to remember is that, whatever choice we make, there will be consequences. That's what many forget. There will be a cause and effect. The bigger the decision, the bigger the consequence. Jennifer Martin's story is tragic. She chose drugs, and her killers chose murder. Each was a deliberate act that resulted in devastating, ongoing consequences, not only for those involved, but for those around them. Choose wisely in all you do. Good choices result in good consequence. Bad choices bring bad consequences.

Iron Theme:
- Every Choice Has a Consequence.

Action Steps:
- Take time to think through all of the possible consequences of your decisions before you make your choice.
- Involve those who care for you in your decision-making. Listen to what they say.
- Once you make a choice, you own it. Take responsibility.

How It Started

●●●

We are all born with gifts and talents. Some more than others, but gifts nonetheless. Some are discovered early in life, while others may take time to germinate. One of mine took only eight years to surface.

In the summer between third and fourth grades, my sister won a prize for tossing a Ping-Pong ball into the glass globe at the Shiawassee County Fair. Her prize? A half-dead goldfish from a tattooed, chain-smoking carnie. It didn't take long for my sister to realize that having one little globe with a fish wasn't good enough; now she wanted a real fish tank and way more fish. Without batting an eye, my parents agreed. I wasn't surprised.

I felt left out. Empty-handed and determined to have a pet of my own, I formulated a plan.

"Hey, Pop, if Kathy gets a fish tank with more fish, can I get a horse?"

At the time, I felt the two were comparable. How could a dad say no to such a reasonable request? He didn't. Instead, he offered me a challenge I'm sure he never thought his eight-year-old son would have the commitment and ingenuity to pull off.

"Sure, Dude! If you save enough money, you can get whatever you want." His words set me up for a lifetime of opportunity.

"Sweet! I'm gonna buy a horse." That day I embarked on my two-year, money-hustling, cash-saving adventure. Soon after I got started, my mom took me to the Genesee Bank to open a savings account. It wasn't long before I began to hunt for discarded beer and pop cans on the side of the streets.

We lived three miles from a golf course. I walked the entire length of the course, collecting every errant ball I could find. I scrubbed those suckers up and sold them by the dozen to golfers at my dad's work. The cash began rolling in.

Although that was all good, the most successful business I created was selling gum at Reid Elementary School. I made a ton of money from that one. Every day after school, either my parents or one of my older brothers would drive me to Perry's Drug Store in Grand Blanc, Michigan. I picked up the most novel gum products on the market: watermelon Bubbalicious, grape Bubble Yum, or whatever had the highest demand. A pack of five pieces cost me thirty-five cents. I sold each piece for a quarter—a 300 percent markup! I used an old cigar box to hold my inventory, and I sold out nearly every morning before 9 a.m. It was an incredible sales experience.

One of my best customers was one of the most unfortunate kids in the school, Jason Wheeler. He struggled in almost every area, but he and I were friends, and I always looked out for him. It wasn't uncommon for him to eat my gum for lunch. He loved it.

The big break in my business came when I was in fifth grade, and the gum gurus came out with Tube Gum. It was genius—the hottest thing to ever hit the sugar market shelves, in my young opinion. I could buy a tube for fifty-five cents and sell it for a buck. Not as big of a markup as the singles, but I made up for that in volume. It didn't matter how many tubes I had. I sold out the first hour of every day. I sold it on the bus, on the sidewalk, at my locker, and even had a clandestine way of continuing to sell during class. If the demand was there, I made sure to seize the deal. I learned that success occurs when preparation and opportunity intersect, and I was there to catch it.

Unfortunately, like everything else, what goes up must come down. Teachers and other school staff members never minded the fresh scent of melon and grape, but Tube Gum had a smell unique to itself, and it was potent! It must have been, because for gum to be soft enough to shove inside a tube, the chemicals in it had to have been scientific marvels. The more tubes I sold, the stronger the smell. I am not joking when I say that there were classes where more than half the students would be squeezing and chewing my gum at the same time.

The time came when the teachers couldn't stand the smell any longer, and they began to ask questions. My empire was about to crumble at the hands of Roy Stacey, the school principal. He was a suited giant with a bald head and a pointed nose, a true Sherlock Holmes look-alike. Nobody went to Mr. Stacey unless he or she was about to get the death penalty. There is no doubt in my mind that Roy Stacey had been installed at the school to scare kids into obedience, and he was just the man for the job.

One morning, I had not yet sold out and had been forced to use my locker for the overflow inventory. The classroom speaker crackled and a voice spoke, "Mrs. Kuehn, please send Christopher Swanson to the office."

My head snapped up, and I'm sure I turned at least two shades paler.

"Yes, ma'am," said my teacher. "Christopher, you need to go."

My journey to the office seemed to last for miles. I walked into the principal's outer office where his secretary sat. She motioned for me to go directly into his office.

"Good grief, let's not rush this," I thought.

"Take a seat, Christopher."

Mr. Stacey stood over me like a storm cloud. That was intimidation, let me tell you! "Chris, are you selling gum at school?"

How could I dispute it? The entire school smelled like a tube gum factory. "Yes, sir."

"Do you have any with you today?"

I could not lie. "Yes sir, it's in my locker."

Upon hearing my confession, Mr. Stacey did the unthinkable. He made me take him to my warehouse where he confiscated every last bit of the gum. He shut me down.

For a moment, I felt like that was the end of my business venture. But suddenly, there was a glimmer of hope. I was crushed, as you can imagine, and I wanted to respect Mr. Stacey and never sell gum at school again. Then it occurred to me that he hadn't said I couldn't sell the items outside of school, so I moved my operation to the buses!

After two years of creating multiple streams of income, the day came. It was a sunny Saturday morning when I ran to the driveway and found the *Flint Journal* lying on the gravel driveway. Grabbing it and running into the house, I went directly to the classifieds. I had been scanning them for weeks, looking for an affordable horse, and suddenly there it was. *For Sale, a brown Welsh pony named Molly. Seven years old. Great with kids and adults. $150.00, $40.00 for the saddle and bridle.*

I had saved for two years, never taking a dime out of my account, and I had accumulated $200. I ran to my parents and showed them the ad. They were shocked. How could they back out now? They had told me to save for a horse and I had.

That day, a ten-year-old little boy businessman bought his dream pony and supplies for $190. With that, came a life lesson worth millions.

I learned that whatever Chris Swanson committed to, he would put forth the effort needed to achieve it.

That life lesson was the first of many that began my transformation from *Tinman to IRONMAN*. Although I wouldn't recognize it for nearly twenty years, that was how it started.

Iron theme:
- Stay Focused.

Action Steps

- Decide upon a specific goal and write it down.
- Tell what you are doing; this builds accountability.
- Do something every day, even if it's small, that takes you closer to your end goal.

THAT STUPID PRACTICE JERSEY

● ● ●

There are two ways to learn a hard lesson in life. The first is from our mistakes. The second, and the better alternative, is to learn from someone else's errors.

The fall was upon us and football was in the air. I was in the eighth grade and felt as awkward as most boys do at that age. Parts of my body were growing faster than others, my skin was far from smooth, the girls in school were becoming women, and I was stuck between a boy and a man. Life for an eighth grader was traumatizing. One afternoon, as I sat in Mr. Sellar's World History class, the crackle of the PA system gave notice to all that we were about to hear an announcement. As the invisible announcer began his opener, it didn't take me long to realize this was not a normal announcement, but a sales pitch. The salesman was the athletic director.

"May I have your attention please?" he began.

I had always thought that was a dumb question. In school, you *had* to give the person speaking your attention, even if you didn't want to.

The voice continued. "We're selling practice jerseys for the football team, and the price is eight dollars. If would like to purchase a jersey, you can bring your money to the office, and they will order your size." Before the PA clicked off, I had already decided to pick up my own jersey.

The next day, I brought my money and handed it to the office secretary. She took it with a smile and assured me they would be delivered in a few days. She was right. In less than a week, I had my blue and gold Goodrich Martian practice jersey in hand. As anyone who has ever attended school knows, Fridays are game days. Everyone wears their jerseys to show their involvement and support of the team, and I was no exception. I awoke the morning of the first game, put my jeans on, and pulled my new jersey over my ears. I wore it on the bus, into the school, and down the halls, beaming with pride and honor.

Within seconds, my world began to crash around me. Humiliation and regret filled my veins. I felt as though I was the laughingstock of the school, and perhaps, they were right. Buying the jersey was not the problem. Wearing the jersey was not the problem. The problem was that I bought and wore the jersey, and I wasn't even on the team! One kid after another asked me why I was wearing a jersey if I wasn't playing football. Those on the team glared at me, knowing I was wearing the colors, but that I had never set foot on the field. Even though my intentions were pure and all I wanted was to wear the jersey, it never occurred to me what the perception would be. I had to junk the jersey as fast as possible. The only problem was that I had no other shirt to wear, so I was forced to wear it the entire day. Like a scarlet letter on my chest, I walked the halls in shame. As the day came to an end, I counted the seconds. All I wanted to do was get home and rip that jersey off my body.

I learned that day to never pretend to be something you are not. Don't take credit for others' success and accomplishments. Earn the right to wear your own jersey with pride. Otherwise, your creditability will be shot. That was the last day I ever wore that stupid practice jersey.

Iron Theme:
- Be You!

Action Steps:
- Know and believe that you are one-of-a-kind. Nobody in the entire world is exactly like you.
- You are capable of doing *whatever* it is that you put your mind to.
- When you set your mind, you carve out your own path. Don't depend on others to do this for you.

CALL TO CRY

● ● ●

I grew up as the youngest of four kids to middle-class parents who, to my knowledge, never played competitive sports. My older siblings all followed suit, and then I came along. I was different in more ways than one. I started my athletic career playing tee-ball, which over the years, led to fast pitch. I played six years in a summer youth league. But the sixth year was the highlight year. I shared the title of "Home Run King" with another kid, Jason Sabedra. He and I were on different teams, but our paths often crossed. It was flattering as a young player to be known for such an accomplishment among my peers.

When I turned 13, my family moved from the only town I knew, 15 miles west. I went from being a farm kid in a school of 400 to living on a postage stamp lot in a racially diverse subdivision and attending a school of 2,800.

I started my freshman year slowly building a level of comfort in that new environment. I had to either adapt or get crushed. The winter came and went, and after the deep freeze of Michigan, spring came, which meant baseball. Returning to the game was priority number one for me. It wasn't long before the tryout notices hit the school walls, and I was all over it. Tryouts commenced and I played each position. I batted, fielded, and threw the ball. It was glorious. Throughout the week, I noticed an unusual interaction between the other players and the coach. They had a level of confidence that I never felt. It wasn't until much later that I realized they had all grown up playing ball together. I was the outsider.

The weekend came, and the coach's picks for the team were to be posted by nine o'clock Monday morning. The ole' "Home Run King" was pretty confident. Monday arrived and the minutes of the morning class went by as if time were standing still. The bell rang, and off I went to the south end of the school where the list was to be posted on the window of the athletic office. I rounded the corner to see my fellow baseball recruits already reading their places on the 1986 Grand Blanc High School freshmen baseball team. I lined up at the back of the pack because the front spots had been taken by the early spectators. I scanned the memo up and down, reading the names one by one. Finally I found it: CHRIS SWANSON. I had made the team! At that moment, I was energized and affirmed as the new kid on the block who could play ball. There was just one problem.

Upon closer examination, I saw there were actually two lists. The first was labeled "Selected" and the other was labeled "Not Selected." I was on the second list. I had been cut! The sensation of failure and rejection was numbing. I had to hold it together in that setting where crying was a definite sign of weakness. I can still feel my heart racing and the fist-sized lump that took up residence in my throat. All I wanted was comfort. I needed my dad. I walked away and found the closest phone I could find, then called my dad's office.

Anticipating the results that morning, he opened with, "Well, did you make it?" That was all it took. I lost it and sobbed uncontrollably, still trying desperately not to be noticed by the other students. I felt like such a loser—not because I was crying but because I was embarrassed. As bad as he wanted to, my dad couldn't take the sting of defeat from me. He could only listen. In hindsight, that's all I really wanted. Sometimes, just listening to a crying heart is the best medicine. Never be afraid to let it go and cry out to those who love you. That's true courage. I honestly don't remember how the conversation progressed or how it ended. But I do know this: it was the last time I competed for over fourteen years.

I have no excuse for choosing not to fight back. Maybe it was immaturity, a lack of belief in myself, or the fact that I was not encouraged by those closest to me. But one thing is for sure, I made the choice not to come back, practice harder, hit better, and turn defeat into victory. It cost me some of the greatest years of my childhood. I missed out on high school sports and all that surrounded them. Why? Because I was humiliated. I quit. I chose not to fight. I took the coward's road. I was the only one to blame.

Don't give up when you lose a battle. If you lose the battle, that doesn't mean you've lost the war. Defeat is character building and adds layers to the uniform of thick skin. When you stumble, you learn. Benjamin Franklin wrote, "Pain instructs."

I remind myself often that life will hurt and people will disappoint. Get over it! Warriors win.

I reflect back to that day and the call I made to my dad. What would have happened if I had gone back the next spring and worked harder, trained longer? Would I have ended up in professional sports, knowing now my Ironman mentality?

What I do know is that I should never have ended my dream to play baseball and called to cry.

Iron Theme:
- Turn Defeat into Victory!

Action Steps:
- Identify where you went wrong.
- Find a way to fix what went wrong, if possible.
- Repeat steps 1 and 2 for the rest of your life.

A HUGE PILE OF GOO

●●●

New Year's Day 2000. I was at my house and saw something that freaked me out enough to change my life forever.

The Michigan winter was in full force, and although it wasn't late, darkness had set in. "Guess I'll go to bed early tonight," I told my wife.

The soft bed with its puffy, brown comforter called my name as I walked up the stairs of our two-story house. A hall window framed the wintery setting, with streetlights illuminating big snowflakes drifting lazily toward the ground. Our quiet subdivision provided a safe haven from the crime-filled city where I spent most of my days.

I started to walk toward the shower attached to our bedroom when I suddenly glimpsed the intruder out of the corner of my eye. My heart raced, and I stopped breathing for a second. Our eyes locked, and we both froze in place. Fear gripped me as much as him. I could see it on his face.

He was my height and overweight. With little muscle tone, his rounded shoulders aged him. I thought to myself, "What the heck! I know this guy." The intruder that reflected back at me in my full-length mirror was me.

What had I become? The man who stood before me had lost his physically commanding presence.

Anger and discouragement coursed through me.

I looked myself in the eyes and vowed to make a change in my life that very second.

I hadn't made any New Year's resolutions as I had never been a resolution guy. I used to laugh at those who made them, knowing the failure rate was so high. I'd wait for them to fail—and most did. That day, though, I made my very first one: I was going to *get* in shape rather than *be* a shape.

In uniform, I could hide my physical weaknesses. But like so many secrets we try to hide, the problem was still there underneath the surface. I decided the best thing to do was to live a life with nothing to hide. Nothing to hide—nothing to fear!

It had been fourteen years since I took competing seriously. I had worked seven years at the sheriff's office. Holidays had come and gone, and I had done what a lot of us do: I had made a lifestyle of consuming more calories than my body burned.

My lack of discipline was not just during the holidays; I ate like a horse every day.

Just thinking about what I used to pack in my lunch makes me want to puke in my mouth. A typical lunch back then included two peanut butter and jelly sandwiches on white bread (yes, fat and sugar lathered on the worst possible bread ever sold). For good measure, I threw in barbecue potato chips, a juice box, *Little Debbie Swiss Cake*

Rolls, and an oatmeal pie for my daily fiber intake. There was nothing healthy in this smorgasbord of fatness, and I ate this nearly every day for years.

I can remember running lights and sirens while responding to a cardiac arrest victim and going 110 mph in my cruiser, steering with my left hand and digging out a handful of chips with my right. That spelled stupid in so many ways.

I knew I had to face my food demons. Nobody was going to lose the weight or build my body but me.

I remembered that eight-year-old boy who saved for two years to buy a pony. I knew tenacity still lived under all my layers of laziness. If I could discipline myself to reach a goal at that young age, I sure as heck could do it now.

I started to search for a plan and a goal. I needed an incentive and a deadline. I learned about the November 2000 NPC Natural Bodybuilding show in Flint, Michigan. The National Physique Committee (NPC) bills itself as "the premier amateur physique organization in the world."

I would do what Arnold Schwarzenegger did to gain his greatness and compete in a bodybuilding contest. I decided that if I was going to stand on stage in bikini trunks, I better not look like a pork sausage. I'd better get with the program and be ready.

I used that show to give me a push every day. I questioned if what I was doing at that moment was taking me closer to or farther from the stage. I kept the vision of me standing on that stage in front of me as I made choices about diet, training, cardio and weight lifting.

I took instruction and implemented the Bill Phillips' "Body for Life" program and soon the weight dropped off, revealing lean muscle.

I have recommended and will continue to recommend the "Body for Life," "Insanity," and "P90X" programs to anybody who desires a physical transformation. I use them to this day. Interestingly enough, I discovered that everybody has abdominal muscles but, in order to see them, you have to lose the insulation that surrounds them. Over time, my "no-pack" transformed into a two-pack—a four-pack—and then a six-pack! I trained harder, ate better, and became more focused as the contest drew near.

November 8, 2000. Pre-judging started around nine in the morning and ended at noon. Each competitor competed individually. There was no fancy music, only mandatory poses and the judges' scorecards. Never underestimate the amount of effort it takes to hold a pose for three minutes. I compare it to suicide sprints on a hot and humid summer day.

Once the pre-judging was complete, the competitors broke for the afternoon and returned in the evening for the night show. Then we posed with music, crowds, and tons of energy. The night was clearly much more enjoyable than the day. Once the posing was complete, it was time for the results. Scores didn't matter to me. I had already won in my head. I had come from such a dark place that New Year's night to the bright lights of the stage, a journey that had required hard work, dedication, sacrifice, and broccoli—lots of broccoli. I took third place and won a two-foot trophy. That show gave me the incentive to participate in three more natural bodybuilding shows. I loved the discipline.

From that point on, I knew I couldn't ever take my foot off the pedal and slide back into my old habits. Fad diets and a return to my previous lifestyle were not an option. I continued to force myself to step out of my comfort zone and finish five marathons and three Ironman competitions.

I created a lifestyle of personal development for myself. An underdog can become an alpha dog. I'm proof of that. I had no special gifts; I found no easy tricks to get it done. I did it all "naturally" with no drugs or muscle supplements. I made a decision, set goals, and stuck to the plan. You are no exception. If you see yourself in the mirror and feel the same way I felt, make the decision to change, and pick a goal to keep you motivated.

Don't be like me and one day look into the mirror and see a huge pile of goo.

Iron Theme:
- Take Pride in Your Body.

Action Steps:
- Make a decision to get control of your body. Diet. Get rid of alcohol, cigarettes, drugs, etc.
- Find a plan, a program, or a trainer/coach to help you through to success.
- Stick with the plan! Diets cannot be sustained; fad workouts don't last. This has to be a *lifestyle change —* and you've got to work for it!

Sometimes, You Need to Just Shut Up and Eat Your Peas

●●●

I hate peas. In fact, when I got married, I made my wife promise to never buy, store, cook, or serve green peas. Yes, I realize they are good for you, but I could find other options. Sometimes, however, getting to where we want to be requires doing things we don't like doing. There is a huge difference in training for a fall marathon in Michigan than a spring marathon in Michigan. That difference is about sixty degrees.

Fall marathons allowed for the luxury of warmer weather throughout the training season and beautiful trees that blossomed with the greenest of leaves. Training took place on longer days filled with natural light from the hot sun and the early morning sound of birds as they too awake to the day's sunlight. Not so for the spring marathon. For me, training started January 1. By then, the trees were naked and clouds filled the sky way more often than the sun ever did. Birds didn't sing, clear roads were history, and the bitter cold wind chill could make a grown man cry. It was not uncommon to have less than 10 hours of daylight for the first three months of training.

Now that wouldn't seem so oppressive if you had all day to train. But the average Joe or Sue doesn't. Most of these people work hard during the day. Nights are filled with basketball, swim meets, wrestling, and piano. Not to mention schoolwork, church, and if you're lucky enough to be in school yourself, add studies to the pile. The question is, if you are training for an event, should those distractions stop you? Could you be called a champion if you were the king of excuses? On game day, would anybody care if you had so much going on that you were ill-prepared to complete? Nope! If you failed, you were roadkill, and you would need to get out of the way.

My second marathon took place the fourth week of May. My training style included a lot of speed drills on weekdays and a long distance run every other weekend. The long distance runs started at a minimum of 10 miles and went up by one to two miles every two weeks. I will never forget those mornings, getting up before everyone in the house. I would step out of bed and look back at the impression in the mattress that I had formed throughout the night. The temperature difference between my warm cocoon and the ambient room air was about 15 degrees. My stiffened body stumbled to the bathroom for the morning hydration release. As nature took its course, I inevitably started to wonder, *Why? Why am I the only idiot up? What is the point of dressing in layers, strapping on my running shoes, hat, warm gloves, and outer jacket, only to drive to meet other idiots wearing the same goofy clothes and running for hours?*

The answer was so clear. If it were easy, everybody would do it.

That's all it is. You have to have the willpower to do what your body doesn't want you to do, in order to feed the spirit what it craves.

It's like those days your mom sat you down in a big fluffy diaper. You couldn't speak the language, you slept whenever and wherever you wanted, like you were born into Club Med. In order to stay strong and healthy, your caregiver would make some stupid noises, wrinkle her face, and scoop up a big ole' spoonful of green vegetable puree. For me, I hated peas then, and I still do today. But mom knew what was best for me.

Now it's your turn. You need to set the goal, carry out the training program, and do what is best for you. Stay committed, even when the odds are stacked against you and training hurts. Do what it takes. Sometimes you need to just shut up and eat your peas.

Iron Theme:
- Have Willpower.

Action Steps:
- Convince yourself that if what you want requires sacrifice, you will do what it takes.
- Be all in.
- What's good for you may not "taste" so great; do it anyway.

BOYS MAKE EXCUSES; MEN MAKE CHANGES

●●●

Why is it that when we can't get something done—win the game, catch a break, or obtain a certain level of success—our first inclination is to quickly find an excuse and pass the blame? Without a doubt, this has become a habit in today's culture that has busted up marriages, divided families, and destroyed dreams. Folks start out with the best of intentions, only to fall off the course over time. Once they gain their composure, here come the excuses.

As a police interrogator, my job is to sit across from the criminal and formulate both a report and a theme. With those two objectives in mind, my goal is to make the suspect so comfortable that they confess to their criminal action.

It was Labor Day 2003, a bright and beautiful Saturday morning. I was the on-call detective that weekend, which meant if anything went down, I would be called. The morning birds sang and the sun radiated over the city. Just twenty miles north of my downtown office, two male suspects decided to enter a gas station convenience center, hold the clerk at gun point, and steal as many cartons of cigarettes and as much money as they could shove into their pockets.

The two waited in the lot for any customers to disappear, and then they struck. Black hoodies covering their faces, they entered the glass enclosure with a short-barreled shotgun and hollered at the clerk, "Get down!" Without hesitation, the clerk dropped to the floor. One of the suspects jumped the counter, stuck the barrel of the gun in her face, and demanded she open the cash drawer. With trembling fingers, she managed to open the register, allowing the turds full access to whatever they wanted. The terrified clerk cowered in the corner as cash and change were emptied from the till. Seconds felt like hours.

As the greedy pair moved from the cash register to the cigarette display, something unexpected occurred. A customer showed up. Out of habit, the unsuspecting customer went to grab the door of the store as he had so many times before and found it locked. He looked inside and saw the store clerk hiding and cowering in the corner. He immediately retreated to his car for safety and called 911.

Inside, the two suspects realized what was happening. Being the cowards they were, their toughness turned to fear when they realized their gig was up. They left the clerk, ran to the back of the service center, and looked for a place to hide. After running up the stairs to the second floor, they scrambled into the rafters, hoping to conceal themselves. Within seconds of the 911 call, cruisers started to respond to the armed robbery call. They filled the lot and surrounded all exits.

The clerk ran to the locked door and escaped after turning the tumbler lock to her freedom. The only ones left inside the store were the two suspects, both armed with weapons. In a scenario like that, with such an open space, one of the best tools for the police to use has four legs and bites. The K-9 unit was sent in and within seconds, the dog had found his targets hiding among a stack of car tires on the mezzanine above. They screamed as the K-9 snapped at them ferociously. Compliance was an understatement. Weapons were no match against the dog. Police swarmed the interior, and both suspects were taken into custody.

There are two reasons I know so much about what happened that Saturday morning. The first is because the store had a surveillance video. Secondly, I took the confession of both suspects.

Both felons had grown up in the same neighborhood. I'm sure they had it tough growing up, with poverty and violence from the cradle to the present. One can only imagine what horrible things go on behind the doors of dope houses and in the alleys, and these guys lived it. I interrogated them individually and could clearly see that one was the mastermind and the other was the knucklehead. The ringleader went by "Sekou" (C-Q) on the street.

Sekou's story forced me to look at the boys' crime in a different light. I couldn't justify it, but I could rationalize it. The interview started with, "Yo dawg, check this out. I been smellin' grillin' ribs and burgers all weekend, and I was hungry. I'm tired of being hungry. It's a holiday and everybody in the hood be eatin' like a king, and I had nothing. I did what I had to do, and I robbed that 'b' and

I'm sorry for what I did, but I'm tired of being hungry." His head slumped forward, and a small trickle of tears flowed toward his chin. The room went so silent that I could almost hear our heartbeats. Remorse flooded through me.

His confession took only seconds. No way do I dismiss the criminal act of the offenders, but let me make it clear that if you do this job long enough, you will empathize with them from time to time. I never grew up in the city with dope dealers as neighbors. I've never fallen asleep with an empty belly twisted in hunger pangs. I've never walked to school not knowing what I was going to eat for lunch, if anything. Listening to that guy was sad, but I still had to finish my job. Once Sekou described to me everything that had happened that morning, I made sure he knew I would be seeking felony warrants for armed robbery and felony firearm. That, I could not change, but I could feel their pain.

I have never crossed paths with Sekou or his partner again; they both pleaded guilty and were sentenced to fifteen years in prison. My hope is that this epic event in their lives drives them to stop blaming the world for their circumstances and fight to be difference makers.

Sadly, this victim mentality keeps champions from achieving greatness every day. Never forget: boys make excuses; men make changes. Which one are you?

Iron Theme:
- No Excuses; Make Changes!

Action Steps:
- Stop blaming others.
- Decide that you are no longer chained to your past and break the trend.
- Take responsibility and *choose* to be different.

WORTHLESS CUP OF MUD

● ● ●

Whenever I commit to an athletic competition, no matter the distance, I count the days leading up to the start. I do it to make sure I am doing something, big or small, every day to ensure that I am prepared. Standing at any start line and not being properly prepared is tragic. Preparation means *training*!

I set each Ironman goal in stone nearly two years out. That way, with each day that passes, I have motivation to train and to work like a dog, even during the times when my body says, "No!" My heart screams, "Go!" Those are the days that make the champion.

Training and competing are much like living life every day. In both scenarios, the athlete can choose to either walk the sidelines or jump into the ring, to train hard or lie around like a slug. If the choice is to play it safe, make no mistake, there will come a day the shroud of regret and shame will be your casket and your shattered dreams the pallbearers.

Conversely, if you *choose* to compete and finish what you set out to do, you will have proven yourself by having the courage to get muddy. Making the choice to succeed in any circumstance will require an investment on your part. Not from your parents, your spouse, or your coworkers, but from *you*. The investment must come from you alone! If you want success, ask yourself, "What will it cost me?" and "Am I willing to pay the price?"

Think of something that you value deeply. Maybe it's your family, your finances, or your friends. In order for that area of your life to prosper at the highest level, you need to invest in it. That's the key. But it's what you put into it that determines its success.

What's important to you is like a glass of water. Picture a spotless glass filled with crystal clear water. Beads of condensation form on the outside as the excess moisture rolls from the top to the bottom, forming a ring. Surrounding that glass are containers of other ingredients you have at your disposal: sugar, salt, food coloring, and nasty dirt. As you work toward your goal, you make choices as to what you will add to that pure glass of water. If you invest in sugar, the water will become sweet to the taste. If you choose to add salt, you have made a choice to season your water. If you add coloring, you make your cool glass of water a beautiful new shade, already sweetly seasoned.

Now, what happens to the clear water if you choose to add the dirt? Or worse yet, allow someone else to pack it full of the nasty sludge? Your once crystal clear glass of water is now changed forever, filled with the soils of failure, resentment, or maybe fear. The more dirt that is added, the faster your glass is forever turned into mud.

That's the power of preparation. Where are you putting your energy? What are you adding to those things that are so important to you? Make the decision to train every day toward reaching your goals. Constantly ask yourself if what you are doing is taking you closer to, or further from, where you want to be. It will take time and hard work. Remember the stonecutter's investment: *"When nothing seems to help, I look at a stonecutter hammering away at his rock perhaps a hundred times without so much as a crack showing. Yet, at the hundred and first blow, the giant structure will split in two, and I know it was not that blow that split the stone, but all he had hammered before..."* (Jacob Riis).

Champions invest daily.

Now go add the sweetener to your life or someone else's. Go make something you value beautiful. If all you add to your glass of life is the dirt, eventually all it will be is a worthless cup of mud!

Iron Theme:
- Prepare and Train.

Action Steps:
- Small investments always pay off over time.
- Decide what you put into your life daily will only be helpful and never harmful.
- Never let anyone stand in the way of your progress.

TRAILER TRASH

●●●

I was a young police officer, not having more than a few months under my belt, and had been married for two years with no kids. Still naïve to the ways of the world, I was working 2nd shift patrol when a call came in from dispatch regarding a domestic fight in the Maple Grove Trailer Park. I had only been to a few domestic fight calls, and I responded along with a Burton City officer. Within minutes, the two of us arrived and located the trailer involved. Although I was a rookie, I still knew enough to arrive quietly to the scene; I didn't slam my car door and I approached in stealth mode. This was so those involve in the domestic dispute would not realize we were on the scene, and we could position ourselves in a safe and tactical way.

As we moved closer to the trailer, I could hear screams from the female inside, along with glass breaking and crying. At that point, the two of us ran full tilt to the sound of the screams, and I kicked the door in. To my left I saw the female victim standing in terror. Her eyes were swollen and filled with tears. She was shaking and still screaming. I continued to scan the room and saw to my right, near the kitchen, a thin white male in a green T-shirt and ratted out blue jeans poised to fight. That was a bad decision on his part. Out of pure instinct, the two of us pounced on him, threw him to the ground, and cuffed him. He could beat up a girl, but with us he was no match—he was just a coward. We dragged him to the Burton City cruiser, and while my partner ran his name through the system to check for warrants and criminal history, I went back to the trailer to check on the victim.

Once inside, I could see she was in no better condition than when I left, minus the screaming. When she saw who I was and that the threat was over, she collapsed to the ground, sobbing. I felt so bad for her. Minutes later she regained partial composure. I was able to get her to the kitchen table to sit down and tell me what happened. Word-by-word, detail-by-detail she told me the terror she had experienced. While the world around her was busy going about their day, she was living a nightmare at the hands of a drunk, abusive monster. The more she talked, the easier it became for her to trust me and calm down. Every few moments I had to assure her that he was gone and she was safe. Her tender tears dried up and her gasping relaxed, which allowed her to control her breathing. I gave her the Domestic Victim Impact Statement form to fill out. This statement is critical in order to memorialize what exactly occurred, and it's heavily relied upon for prosecution. Page-by-page she filled in the blanks as I waited with her.

Just then, out of the corner of my eye, I noticed something had been competing for my attention but had not noticed. While the lady was engrossed in writing, I looked down to my right and saw the frightened brown eyes of a five-year-old boy. Quickly, he wrapped his hands around my right leg. He never said a word, he just hugged my leg. Not having my own kids, I was unaware of the child's silent needs. I just figured he was fascinated with my Glock .40 handgun, which is on my right hip, so I did nothing. The woman completed her form, I peeled the boy off my side, and with robotic precision cleared the scene. The coward was taken to jail, and my partner and I returned to the streets to fight another battle.

For whatever reason, the thought of that little boy never crossed my mind until years later when I was holding my own son. I can't tell you where I was or even his age when it hit me. But the memory of that domestic call returned like I was there the day before. I recalled the screams and the smashing glass. I could see the faces. I saw the face of that little boy looking up at me. My heart broke. Even as I write this, I get choked up thinking about what he might have said to me while he clenched my leg. Would he have told me how scared he was? Would he have asked me to hold him and give him comfort? Or maybe that he was assaulted sexually? I will never know because I never took the time to ask. I did nothing. It wasn't because I was unkind or didn't care; I didn't see the need. I didn't go to his level and look him eye to eye and ask him what *he* needs. I didn't give him the protection he deserved. Why? I just didn't know what to do. I didn't see the signs.

I've prayed for that little guy dozens of times since. My prayer is that our Mighty God would forgive my ignorance and have mercy on him; that He would be the comforter I wasn't.

To have an impact in the lives of others requires that you look around. You need to be aware of the needs of others and to invest in them. You can bet since that call, I never miss the opportunity to seek out hurting people. In fact, I pray for opportunities. I would ask that you do the same. People around you are hurting every day. Find them and love on them. It's a lot more than the Trailer Trash did for his family!

Iron Theme:
- Be Tuned in to Others.

Action Steps:
- Seek out those in need.
- Helping others is seldom convenient and rarely cheap. Invest anyway and don't worry about the outcome.
- Focus on the little things that make you selfless instead of selfish.

POP CANS

●●●

Melvin Bonner lives in Flint, Michigan. He goes to work every day, rain or shine. Regardless of how he feels, he grinds it out. When I say every day, that's exactly what I mean. Melvin provides for himself and makes it a point never to count on others to do his work. If you were to see him on the job, you would never see him slack off. He is never short on a supply of smiles or friendly one-liners.

Melvin is a seventy-three-year-old African American who stands 5'7" and weighs about 160 pounds. In the summer, he is seen wearing open-toed sandals, polyester dress pants, and an untucked, short-sleeved dress shirt. When the Michigan winter hits, he starts the day with a blue knit cap to cover his ears, layers of business-casual dress clothes, and usually, gently worn dress shoes that allow him to dig through the wet snow and slush.

I never miss an opportunity when I see him to greet him and ask how he's been. Only once can I recall him having a "bad day." He had just been released from Hurley Hospital post heart attack. His affliction left him with a slight limp and forever dependent on a light-colored wooden cane.

Melvin Bonner is homeless. He digs through hundreds of trash cans throughout the city of Flint, seeking food and drink that others deem as "garbage." Melvin collects the pop cans and, once he drinks the leftover contents, stuffs them into one of his many plastic grocery bags. When his bags overflow, he brings his bounty to the 12th Street Market at S. Saginaw and 12th and returns them to the store owner. With the deposit money, Melvin buys food. Not booze, crack, or smokes, which is much different than the stigma most people assign to the homeless in America. Melvin Bonner buys food to stay alive. As the nights set in, Melvin tells me he sleeps "here or there" at his preferred abandoned homes throughout his route, depending on weather conditions; the colder the air, the more critical the spot. Melvin talks to me without anger, resentment, or shame. In my opinion, he is a man's man. He gets up every day and goes to work. He can't call in because, if he does, he won't eat. He can't complain because no one would listen. He can't quit or else he would die.

You and I can get caught up in the minutia of life and oftentimes forget just how good we have it. My advice? If you ever feel the "life's not fair" poison start to invade your mind and body, remember that your worst day is many times better than someone else's best day.

I'm sure Melvin made bad choices throughout his life and ran into some bad luck along the way. However, I honor him in that, despite his current circumstance, he makes the decision to survive, to fight another day. Are you prepared to fight another day? If it took you having to collect pop cans to survive, would you humble yourself enough to do it? Author and friend Chris Brady writes in his book, *Rascal*:

1)   Life's not fair. It's been that way since the beginning of time.

2)   It will never be fair. So don't hold your breath waiting.

3)   It will be fair to some and totally unfair to others. Pray you're in the first group.

4)   You can't control it, even if you wanted to.

Yes, it is easier to be scared and fear failure than to be courageous and succeed; but I exhort you—be *fearless* and *courageous* anyway. You will never regret it.

Remember, one man's junk is another man's treasure. And treasures, to Melvin Bonner, are dirty old *pop cans*.

Iron Theme:
- Beat Adversity!

Action Steps:
- If you know going into the ring you are going to get hit, *enter* the ring anyway.
- If you get the opportunity to defend your convictions under intense criticism, *defend* anyway.
- If someone attacks you because you choose not to be a part of the majority, but to stand with the minority champions, *stand* anyway.

A Scare Is Worth a Thousand Words

●●●

In late August 2009, I signed up for the Grand Haven Half-Ironman. The black triangle flag whipped in the cool wind just yards from the waterline of Lake Michigan. When this happens, it's because the waves are violent and swimmers should think twice about swimming in this Great Lake. We woke that morning ready to begin the day with a swim, only to find out that race officials were concerned that the risk factor for the swim was too high. That forced them to consider cancelling the swim and adding another run leg in the beginning, which would make it a Run-Bike-Run triathlon. As we awaited their decision, we watched the waves crash the beach. With only minutes to spare before the eight o'clock start, it was announced on the megaphone, "Racers, we have decided to start with the swim in ten minutes. Please come to the start line in order to be counted."

My first thought was, "Why do they need to count us? They know how many registered for the race." Then it hit me; they wanted to make sure that whoever went into the water hopefully came back out alive—not cool! I'm not afraid to admit my nerves were more than on edge and as the count line progressed, I became even more anxious. I'm sure I wasn't alone. Still, after the last triathlete was counted, there was a simultaneous firing of the starter pistol and a mass of wet suits and swim caps hitting the ominous water underneath the stormy gray clouds.

The open water was cold and choppy. When my face hit the ice-cold water, the shock to my skin took my breath away; the vagal response of my body dropped my blood pressure, and I became stiff and rigid. At that point, it became swim to survive. I cut the water with my hands and kicked through the dark waves. I swam through the peaks and valleys of each four-foot wave. Out from the shoreline about 200 yards, I rounded the first corner buoy, turned north, and headed toward the second and last corner buoy. *So far so good,* I thought.

Many times, it takes a minute or so of swimming for me to get into a rhythm. When I do, my movements can be compared to slow dancing, smooth and graceful. With the black flag conditions of the day, however, the slow dance became "mosh pit" dancing. One after another, the waves crashed on top of me, roaring like thunder. I went from a somewhat controlled stroke to a panic! I turned to take a breath, and a wave swept over me, forcing ridiculous amounts of water into my face, my mouth, and my lungs. I instantly started to choke, gasping for breath as if I'd had the wind knocked out of me. I went into a tread position, did a quick look around to get my bearings, and saw only water. No shore, no swimmers, no escape. I was stuck in the middle of the wave, and water was on all sides; I was, for the moment, lost at sea.

In hindsight, I'm sure there were other swimmers close by, but at the time, I couldn't see squat. I thought to myself that this is what drowning feels like. I was alone in the cold, unforgiving water of Great Lake Michigan. I have been swimming for over twenty years, and I have never felt intimidated by the power of nature's water. That changed the day of the race. I freaked out!

Although the waves never relented, after what seemed like an eternity but I'm sure was only a few minutes, I chose to fight. I sat back and treaded water like a mad man. I prayed out loud, "Father God, save me. Calm my body and give me the strength to finish this!" I visualized my beautiful wife and my two boys who knew their dad was an Ironman. I could do this. Just then, a surge of power and peace came over me, compelling me to roll forward on my stomach and frog kick. I complemented my kick with a breaststroke.

Within moments, I was carried on top of a crest and saw a buoy. Like a desert mirage, the finish was still a quarter mile away, but at least I had a heading. I never again took my eyes off the shoreline. I continued to kick and claw my way to the swim finish. As I got closer, I almost broke down in tears, knowing both how fast the plan had gone out the window and that I was alive to tell the story. I rejoiced when my feet hit the soft sandy bottom of the lake. I had made it!

That day I learned never to underestimate the power of that which is bigger than me. I learned to respect what could kill me if I lost my focus and to take nothing for granted.

In the police department, we learn that we need to be lucky and right every time, but the killer only needs to be lucky once.

Lake Michigan proved that to me. It taught me the lesson that a scare is worth a thousand words.

Iron Theme:
- Turn Fear into Focus.

Action Steps:
- Fear is to be respected. Fear what can kill you and don't be stupid.
- When you are overtaken by fear, talk to yourself out loud. Fear stands for *False Evidence Appearing Real*, and you can calm yourself down by reminding yourself of this.
- Get yourself out of a jam one step at a time. Never stop fighting to survive.

THE BUBBLE GUTS

●●●

Not many can say they grew up in jail, but I can. Not as an inmate, but as a Deputy Sheriff. I was hired at age twenty on June 2, 1993, by the sheriff's office in Flint, Michigan. I have spent more time at that place than I did growing up with my parents. It was there that I first learned about the criminal mind. I learned how to break into homes undetected, how to scam credit card companies, and best of all, how to cook crack cocaine on a rusty spoon; these are life lessons a kid raised on a horse farm never thought he would ever learn.

In addition to this vocational training in crime, I learned what prisoners do to pass the time and how they talk behind prison walls. A convicted murderer taught me one of the coolest card tricks I've ever learned called "Little Joe." It uses every card in the deck to tell the story of "Little Joe" who had just been released from prison. He goes back to his hometown with a $50 check to hustle some of the folks out of their money. The trick uses all fifty-two cards in the deck, and I learned to master the trick and still can do it nearly twenty years later. Crowds love it! What you can learn from prisoners is priceless.

In the fall of 1993, I bid to work the fourth floor. That floor is split by two pods, A/B and C/D. I had 4A/B. When you work a floor every day, you get to know the inmates, their habits, and their behavior. Over time, you build a rapport, which helps to keep order throughout the shift. That floor holds 120 of the most heinous criminals in the Flint community.

One day, I was sitting at the duty station watching an inmate approach; the man was crouching forward and holding his stomach with both hands. His face grimaced with each step he took. He leaned his hunched shoulders toward me as he whispered, "Yo, Dep. I need some help. Can you please call medical?"

"What for?" I asked.

"Brother, I got the bubble guts!"

Somewhat sarcastically, I asked him, "What the heck are bubble guts?"

"You know, my stomach, it's killin' me. I'm sick."

I still feel bad thinking how I laughed out loud at that inmate's intestinal tribulation. From that day forward, any time I got sick, I would think about bubble guts and how it hit me with a vengeance.

Years later at *Ironman Kentucky*, I had just completed my first 50-mile bike loop and was on target to an even better second half. For whatever reason, my partner offered me an energy drink, something I had never taken in the past. Rule #1—*Never* try something new on race day. I knew this golden rule and still dismissed its importance. I paid greatly for my arrogance. Within ten miles, I felt like someone had shoved half a pound of gravel in my gut. That led to powerful cramps and nausea. I realized right then that I had given myself the "bubble guts."

With sixty-two miles on the bike and a marathon to go, I could either suck it up or quit. The latter was not an option. Over the next seven hours, neither warm cola nor chicken broth could quell the raging storm. Unable to purge the poisons, I forced myself to finish the race. But I paid the price in the "back end."

There may be times when we get into something we either hadn't trained for or we have not prepared well enough for. That's when the suffering kicks in. You can't avoid it; you have to face the pain. The results of our actions might be uncomfortable, but they usually don't kill us. If you can promise yourself to persevere through every challenge, chances are, you will never fall victim to the bubble guts.

Iron Theme:
- Don't Sweat the Small Stuff.

Action Steps:
- Push through.
- Pain is temporary; victory lasts forever.
- You are not going to die, so relax.

DID YOU GET MY NOTE?

●●●

Marc Ferguson is a fellow police officer at the Grand Blanc Police Department and an amazing athlete. He can eat cartloads of junk and still stay lean. He's about 5'11" and weighs around 165 lbs. Even though he was athletic, he had never run a marathon. One day, he told me he wanted to finish a marathon, and I committed to passing on to him all the knowledge I had gained in order for him to do just that. We trained in the snow, the rain, and the sun; early in the morning and after work. When you are training with someone, you become very close throughout the process. You know what's happening in his life.

After months of training, the day of the marathon was quickly approaching. Marc was getting more excited by the hour. The plan was to meet at 0430 hours at a party store where I would drop off my car and ride the rest of the way with him in a 1993 red Pontiac Sunfire. Everything was on schedule. We met at the spot and drove the forty-five minutes to the race. Traffic was ridiculous. Everybody was scrambling to get a parking spot in time to get all their gear ready, stretch, hit the most disgusting porta-johns you will ever visit, kiss their families good-bye, and make it to the start line. That's where this story begins.

Once Marc and I pulled into a spot on the street and started to get our gear ready, I noticed that he had something very special in his hand. It was a red heart made from school construction paper, and on the inside his wife had written him a beautiful note wishing him love and support. As he read it aloud, I witnessed his pride and joy with every word. Although she couldn't be at the start, she promised to be at the finish line with both his little girls. There is no question, something like that brings calmness to a person and refocuses them on the task ahead. There is power in words.

After his quick read, I had just started to get out of the car when Marc inquired, "Dude, is your wife coming to the race?"

His words hurt. Although my Jamie has been to countless events throughout my career, she was not coming to this one, and an immediate sense of loneliness came over me. "Nope, she can't," I responded, and off to the start we headed.

The morning was clear and brisk. The first seven miles were uneventful, but the next 19.2 were far from it. Marc and I stuck together. I made sure he didn't take off too fast and wasn't holding back at the same time. For runners, it takes a few miles to get into a groove, and then the miles start to fall faster and faster. At mile eight, without warning or explanation, my right foot started to throb. I tried to adjust my running style with no luck.

As the miles progressed, so did the pain. With every step, a sharp sensation shot across my foot from my pinkie toe to my ankle. At mile 14, I lost my first toenail and, as disgusting as it sounds, could feel the fluid from the blisters and blood swishing around inside my right shoe. With all that, I had no option but to continue. 15, 16, ... 24, 26... The pain only got worse. My running gait went from a traditional step to sort of a dead man's shuffle. By that time, Marc had moved way ahead; all I wanted to do was finish.

For the Detroit Marathon, as long as there is no Lions home game, runners can run into the tunnel on Ford Field and finish on the 50-yard line. It took all I had to get to the finish. Family and friends of athletes were there to share the victory. Looking back, it was probably best that my family wasn't there since my foot was so painful. I wouldn't have been much of a good sport anyway.

Once I found Marc, I was introduced to his family, including the author of the heart-shaped note, his wife. It was the first time I had met her, and I could see they were a great fit. After an hour of rehashing the race and Marc reveling in his first successful marathon finish, the two of us began the slow walk to his Sunfire. Of course, my pace was much slower than his as I braced myself whenever I could find a pole or tree on the way.

The drive back wasn't as bad as I had anticipated because I was sitting. As soon as I made it into the garage of my home, I must admit that the fact Marc had been shown so much support gave me an attitude. I realize it was selfish, but when you see someone get showered with attention and you get nothing, it can get under your skin, immature or not. My wife, Jamie, met me at the door, excited to see me. We hugged and exchanged a few words before I made my way up to the shower.

I had already stripped my shoes off, but the socks were a whole different story, let me tell you. Imagine a gory mixture of sweat and blood topped with a detached toenail. That's the surprise I found in my right sock. When I stepped into the shower, the water ran down my body and onto my feet, burning like acid. The shower was the farthest thing from relaxing, but it was necessary. Jumping in and out quickly, I put on a clean set of clothes, threw the socks in the trash and slowly made my way to the couch. I was lying there when my wife came in, wanting to continue part two of our earlier conversation.

I went on a tirade, telling her how terrible it was. "My foot started killing me around mile eight. It only got worse when I got blisters and at the end, I wished you were there." With every intention of making her feel terrible for neglecting me, I continued, "Marc's wife made him a big heart with a sweet message inside. She hid it and when he found it before the race, he was so excited. It would have been nice if you had done something like that." I could see that something was going terribly wrong with each word I spoke. Jamie showed no signs of remorse or defense. Was it *how* I said it, or *what* I said? Eating words never tasted good and, without realizing it, I had just taken an entire mouthful.

"What do you mean you had no support? Did you get my note?" she asked.

"No, I didn't get your note."

"I put it in your shoe."

I was stunned. "What?! Go get my shoe please." Jamie jumped up from the couch, went into the garage, and came back with a nasty, bloody, right running shoe. I reached my hand into the toe and pulled from it a wad of blood-soaked loose-leaf paper that had once held a beautiful message from my bride. I couldn't believe it. She told me she had written the note the night before and put it in my right shoe. Without thinking, I had put my shoes on without noticing the hunk of paper jammed into the toe that had led to a podiatric tragedy. I was torn between gratefulness, anger, and love.

To this day, I always check my shoes as well as all my gear. I make sure everything is accounted for and in working order. I pay much more attention to the small details. In life, you must do the same. It's the small things that can grow to become monumental problems if they persist. I love my wife, but I told her that, for the next fifty years, if she wants to leave me a note, put it in my pocket. "No, I did not get your note!"

Iron Theme:
- Don't Jump to Conclusions!

Action Steps:
- Get all the facts.
- Get the story behind the story.
- Always extend forgiveness.

The Corner Buoy

●●●

Traditionally, triathlons always start with the swim. Prior to the start, athletes line up on the beach and snap mental pictures as they focus on the corner buoys that mark the turnarounds. It's those corner buoys where integrity and deceit intersect.

The corner buoy offers two options: the first is to do the right thing and swim around the outside as the course was designed. The second is to cut the inside corner, shortening your distance to the finish, and avoiding a mass of people. Either option has something in common: nobody is there to watch you chose. It's truly a personal ethical decision. Surprisingly, each time I compete, many people cut the inside corner and chose not to do what is right.

You can get an edge in life by either cheating or by doing the right thing. But by cheating on even the smallest thing, you will never strengthen your character; it will only diminish. President Abraham Lincoln wrote that *character is built by what you and I do when no one is looking*. Many times, our society encourages us to take whatever shortcut we can get, no matter the consequences. If you get bored, get somebody new. If the company doesn't pay you what you're worth, make up for that in other ways. That's how people rationalize bad behavior, i.e., cheating.

Don't do it!

Leaders and warriors are better than that! Don't take shortcuts at the cost of your character. Swim around the corner buoy the way the course was designed. Finish with pride and be able to share the entire victory without skipping parts and demonstrating ethical weakness.

Doing the right thing is not always the easiest thing, but it's still the right thing. Whenever you are confronted with an ethical dilemma, no matter how small it is, you owe it to yourself to ask: Would I be ashamed if what I was doing made the front cover of a national newspaper? If the answer is yes, then you know what to do. For that reason alone, never cut short the corner buoy.

Iron Theme:
- Never Cheat!

Action Steps:
- Don't take the easy way out.
- Cheating in one area causes you to cheat in other areas.
- Don't do in private what you won't do in public.

THE SOCCER MOM

●●●

Have you ever been in a situation when you think that you are "really amazing," then something happens to show you that you are not? This is commonly referred to as "eating humble pie," and it tastes bitter going all the way down.

Louisville, Kentucky, August 29, 2010. I had completed the swim and bike legs of the race and was putting the miles behind me in the run. Although I was hurt and tired, I had no doubt I would be an Ironman once again. Around mile 22, I thought to myself, *I am in great shape, young and laser focused. I am the man.*

Just then, I heard a faint warning over my right shoulder: "On your right." I looked, and at that moment, I ate my first slice of humble pie. I was in the process of being passed by a woman in her mid-40s who could have stood to lose 20–25 pounds. She trotted one step in front of the other, and as she passed, whispered, "Hang in there! You're almost there." And off into the wind she went. I had just been passed by a soccer mom.

I learned two lessons that day:

First, if I ever think that I am the biggest, baddest, and fastest, it's good to remember that there will *always* be someone badder and faster.

Second, don't be fooled by appearances. They are deceiving. Power lies within the heart and mind. It is what others don't see that gives you the victory.

To all the soccer moms around the world, I've held you in great respect since that day. Keep it up!

Iron Theme:
- Check Your Pride.

Action Steps:
- Stay humble.
- Don't judge by appearances.
- Base your success on what *you* can do, not what others do.

DR. STRESS

●●●

Not all stress is bad medicine. The night before competition teaches three lessons: how to handle stress, how to deal with doubt, and what to do when those two things attack at the same time. This is what I have learned from those nights.

Stress is defined as a negative concept that affects one's mental and physical well-being. Stress has a physiological impact; it increases the level of cortisol in the blood, which increases blood pressure by constricting blood vessels, causing heart disease and stroke; that's the bad stress.

But good stress wins battles. It makes champions and builds greatness. Without stress, there would be no need for the courage to fight the fight. There is no question that good stress invades your body prior to a competition. That's what is supposed to happen at that point. Good stress creates hunger, and hunger brings victory. When you feel overwhelmed, it's time to perform. Go accomplish what you set out to do. Compete, fight, speak, and feed the hunger.

Doubt is uncertainty. The most effective way to remove doubt is to reflect on past victories and dismiss it. We forget just how good we are many times. We forget the "I did it" moments of our personal past that can remind us that we've been here before and won—the I-can-do-this times. If you take the time to inventory your life and consider the mountains of difficulty you overcame, half the battle is already won.

However, when bad stress and doubt form a tag team, you better be prepared for it. The way to do that is to train like a fool. While running Ironman number three, I was hurt and sick. At one point I didn't think I could finish. The stretch between miles 23 and 24 felt ten times longer than it was. Each step was painful as my stomach churned with flu-like symptoms, and I was puking up a slush of Gatorade and phlegm. I forced myself to dismiss my anxiety and remembered how many times I had run between the 23 and 24 mile markers before without quitting.

Dismiss doubt: it's public enemy #1 against success. Embrace good stress as a normal expectation in that it can be used as fuel to win. That's good medicine from Dr. Stress.

Iron Theme:
- Stress Can Be a Friend.

Action Steps:
- Expect doubt and anxiety during critical events.
- Control your responses by reflecting on past victories.

- Find a release for your daily stress or it will eat you up.

I SAW A CHICK WITH ONE LEG

● ● ●

I was lying on the hot white sand of the Panama City Beach, wrapped in a blanket of beautiful, tropical Florida sun. The feeling a day prior to an Ironman—or any competition for that matter—is, in my opinion, worse than anything I ever feel on race day. The anticipation, mixed with uncertainty, is almost unbearable. I always wonder, *Did I train enough? Am I mentally ready? What is the weather going to be like? What if I can't finish?* No matter how prepared, these thoughts plague most competitors.

During one of my many attempts to relax, I noticed something very unusual about the three bodies walking along the beach toward me. Two looked "normal." The other was much different. As they drew closer, I realized what was so different. All three people appeared to be in their mid-20s, athletic, and clearly friends, one guy and two girls.

Something about one of the girls caught my attention. Not her beauty, although she was attractive, not her muscle tone, which was also an asset. But it was the fact that her left leg had been amputated above the knee. What also stood out as much as her missing limb was the shiny silver Ironman competitor bracelet she wore on her left wrist. I glanced down at the identical bracelet on my right wrist. She was registered for the same Ironman that I was. All competitors must wear this bracelet from the moment of check-in until the completion of the race on Sunday. She was a competitor just like me. She didn't look nervous or scared. There was no hint of concern on her face. From the outside, at least, she looked amazing. *Why?* I thought.

As the trio closed the gap, I had to ask, "Hey, what's up?" Not waiting for them to reply, I followed up with a simple, "I gotta know." The girl with the blonde hair and prosthetic leg looked over at me, and her smile lit up her face. I took that as an open invitation to get all the details.

Her name was Deanna Babcock. She was a grad student at North Carolina State. She, like many others, desired to compete in an Ironman. In the summer of 2006, she had committed to gathering two other athletes from college to compete in the *2007 Florida Ironman*. Like all competitors, as the date approached, she increased her training, including her most beloved discipline, swimming. Then, on July 20, 2007, her life changed forever. Her story is best told by a reporter from *The McClatchy-Tribune*, Joe Miller.

Deanna's recollection of the day is fuzzy. She remembers rising early and heading to her 10-foot by 30-foot research plot along Davis Drive. For her graduate thesis in soil sciences, she was testing various materials that could help minimize erosion. She spent the day working in the sun—the temperature peaked that day at 88 degrees—before knocking off about three in the afternoon to get in a swim at N.C. State.

The swim was important. Nine months earlier, Babcock, who had run cross-country as an undergrad at Albion College in Michigan, was watching the Ironman world championships in Kona, Hawaii. *That looks like fun*, she thought. She'd done a couple of sprint triathlons over the summer and performed well, winning her age category in both; an Ironman would just be more—a lot more—of the same.

Deanna joined the N.C. State Triathlon Club, picked an Ironman a year out—*Ironman Florida*, on Nov. 4, 2007—and started training. That training included the *Myrtle Beach Marathon* in February (time: 4 hours, 1 minute), the collegiate nationals triathlon in mid-April, and the *White Lake Triathlon*, an Olympic distance race (just under a mile in the water, 24.8 miles on the bike, a 6.2-mile run) in May.

Her next big test was the *Duke Half Marathon* in September. She needed to swim.

Babcock has to rely on the recollections of others for an account of what happened after she rode her bike to the pool. At some point in her swim, her heart stopped. N.C. State lifeguards pulled her from the water and began CPR. Wake County EMS arrived and had to use a defibrillator three times to revive her.

No one can say for sure how long her heart was stopped. One estimate puts it as long as seven minutes. "It certainly was at least a few minutes," says Dr. Marc Silver, her cardiologist.

"Certainly," he adds, "long enough to do some serious damage."

Bad to Worse

When she arrived at WakeMed, it was feared that Babcock had an enlarged heart, a thickening of the heart muscle. Silver says the condition is more common than generally thought; it only becomes apparent when the heart undergoes an intense workout. When that happens, the heart practically explodes and the situation is almost always fatal.

About 125 athletes younger than 35 die each year from an enlarged heart; among the more prominent recently was 28-year-old marathoner Ryan Shay, who died five miles into an Olympics qualifying event in New York in 2007.

An echocardiogram ruled out an enlarged heart in Babcock's case. A diagnosis would have to wait until other life-threatening problems could be addressed.

When the heart stops pumping and cells stop getting blood, bad things happen quickly. The immediate concern is brain damage. Brain cells start dying after three to four minutes without oxygen. After the brain, the heart and kidneys start to go. With Babcock's heart down for perhaps as long as seven minutes, there was plenty of cause for concern.

That concern immediately focused on her kidneys. The blood-deprived muscle tissue in her legs began leaking an enzyme damaging to the kidneys. Both of them failed and she was put on dialysis.

Then there were her legs. The muscles in her left leg were especially bad; the lack of coursing blood had caused the veins to collapse. Doctors cut the muscle fascia—the thin layer of tissue encasing all muscle—to re-stimulate circulation. Her right leg stabilized; her left worsened. The next day it was amputated about mid-thigh.

Babcock developed pneumonia and was in an induced coma for four weeks, keeping her still for healing purposes.

During that time, though, surprisingly positive signs began to emerge. Her kidneys regained full function, there was no evidence of brain damage, and her right leg improved.

"She is incredibly lucky to be alive," Silver says. "She's a miracle child."

An Aggressive Treatment

Babcock is quick to second that "incredibly lucky to be alive" observation. When I asked her how long it had been since the incident, she replied, "My six-month anniversary of not dying was two days ago. We went out and celebrated with refined sugar."

She's quick to second the "miracle" thing as well including, in part, the technology that saved her life and promises to get it close to where it was before July 20. There were other miracles though, too.

Miracle One: The reason Babcock survived as long as she did without a heartbeat was because of a procedure called induced hypothermia, being used with increased aggressiveness by WakeMed. Induced hypothermia involves dropping body temperature through ice packs and an injection of an icy saline solution via a catheter into balloons placed under the skin.

"The target temperature is 91.4 degrees," says Eric Reyer, a nurse with WakeMed who's involved in the hospital's induced hypothermia program. Cells in a chilled body require significantly less oxygen to survive so the process prevents damage from spreading.

The procedure has been in use for several years, but gained widespread attention in September 2007 when Buffalo Bills tight end Kevin Everett suffered a severe blow to his spinal column, the type of injury that often results in paralysis. To the doctor's credit he had induced hypothermia, due to the fact that three months later, he exhibited few signs of his injury.

Miracle Two: Silver still isn't sure what caused Babcock's heart to stop, but the current thinking is that it was caused by an enlarged right ventricle, something she would have been born with. If the ventricle improves, then Silver will scratch that diagnosis as a genetic condition that can't get better on its own, and he will look elsewhere.

Regardless, Babcock will keep the implantable cardiac defibrillator inserted under her left collarbone. It's a tiny, battery-operated device that, should Babcock's heart stop again, will deliver an electric jolt to jump-start it.

Miracles one and two were life-saving. Miracle three had more to do with saving Babcock's spirit.

Seeking a High-tech Leg

Just because Sarah Reinertsen has a Vari-Flex Total Knee 2100 doesn't mean every above-knee amputee triathlete has to have one, does it?

"Well, yes," says Babcock.

Long gone are the days of stiff wooden legs for amputees. Today's technology makes it possible for amputees to compete at the highest level ....When she left WakeMed in October, she checked out with a basic leg. "It's good for cycling," Babcock says.

Shortly thereafter—after filling out an extensive questionnaire about what she would do with the leg—she got a more sophisticated C-Leg, which has more range of movement.

"It's good for walking," she says. Not so for running. The knee joint works well, but the ankle joint doesn't respond quickly enough. A carbon blade-type foot device would be ideal. Just one problem.

"Those legs can cost, like, $50,000," says Babcock, which is much more than her insurance is willing to pay. So, in November, she made a grant proposal to the San Diego-based Challenged Athletes Foundation. Among other things, the Foundation awards money (about $784,000 in fiscal 2005-06) to help challenged athletes compete. Babcock is waiting to hear back on her request.

In the meantime, she's swimming about 1,200 yards at the Y two times a week and learning to ride a bike again, mostly on a stationary bike in the gym, where she's working on the mechanics of her stroke. Last week, she got outside and rode 12 miles on the American Tobacco Trail. "That went pretty good," she says.

The walking—which will segue into running—is going more slowly. At a session one morning at WakeMed's outpatient rehab, therapist Hannah Dewitt wasted little of her 30 minutes with Babcock. She assessed Babcock's gait on the treadmill for five minutes, had Babcock walk sidewise for another couple of minutes, then ran Babcock through a series of strength and balancing exercises designed to build core muscles and help Babcock establish greater range with her new leg.

Walking is still a chore, Babcock acknowledges. "I do 10 minutes on a treadmill at zero incline, and I'm tired." The carbon blade leg will obviously help, but grant or no, Babcock will keep training. "I don't want to be an active amputee," she says. "I want to be an active person."[1]

Three months later, Deanna Babcock was standing in front of me. I thought to myself, *Who am I to get caught up in doubt and anxiety after personally meeting a person like Deanna?*

The conversation ended, and I told her how awesome she was, and I thanked her for openly sharing it with me. Within minutes, that human inspiration and her two companions disappeared into the sunny Florida horizon.

Even though she had been dealt a life-altering blow over which she had no control, had lost her leg from the complications, and had been forced to the sidelines only to cheer and encourage everybody else, she was there. She wasn't able to compete, but she was there to support others. In my mind, she was an *Ironman finisher* even before the race started. Meeting her was very powerful. It wasn't by accident. Almost instantly, my feelings of fear of the unknown were gone. God showed me a champion in Deanna Babcock, and over the next 24 hours, her impact allowed me to push to the finish of my first Ironman.

Whenever you have an overwhelming sense of defeat, fear, or concern, find people who have overcome what you are feeling. They are out there! If it's death, seek those who have lost people close to them. If it's cancer, talk to survivors. If it's failure, seek out winners. Be motivated by other people's victories; they are so powerful. That day on the beach in Florida, I saw a chick with one leg, and she inspired me forever.

1 – http://www2.ocregister.com/articles/amputee-triathlon-ironman-1981942

Iron Theme:
- Inspiration Drives Motivation!

Action Steps:
- When you embark on the journey, find someone who has been there and hear his or her story.

- You are *never* alone.

Through your victories you can be an inspiration to others.

Subway Napkins

●●●

It was the best swim of my life! It was 2.4 miles in the crystal clear tropical ocean water known as the Gulf of Mexico. Swimming has never been the easiest discipline of the three for me because I find it so boring. No talking, no scenery, and certainly no room for error.

The morning was crisp and clear with the Florida sun just breaking the horizon to our backs. The cannon sounded, and 2,317 swimmers cloned in green swim caps and goggles kicked and clawed at each other, attempting to cut through the great water. Plagued by nervous thoughts of preparedness, it's a fact that even Ironmen can get intimidated by a swim in the unforgiving ocean.

But this day was different. Within the first quarter mile, I felt strong and energized. Eight buoys out, two across, and eight more back to shore. That was the first 1.2 miles. The closer I got to the completion of the first loop, the more I knew I was dialed in the zone. Out of the water in thirty-eight minutes, I ran along the 100 yards of beach and back in for the last 1.2-mile leg. When I jumped back into the water, I did the math in my head and quickly realized now that the herd had thinned, I could have an even better second half.

I swam toward the south buoys, rounded the far corner, and headed for home. I cheered under the water where only the jellyfish in the deep blue sea could witness my enthusiasm, knowing this would be a personal best. It was. Out of the water and onto the timing mat: 1:17:00 hours. That's what makes Ironman so spectacular. You compete against yourself, and I was stoked. One discipline down and two to go.

I ran up the sand to a cheering mob, headed for the "peelers." The peelers are there to rip off your wet suit and keep you on target. They're called "peelers" because all they do is peel the dolphin-like wet suit, which sticks like glue after a swim, off of you. They're a crazy bunch!

Onto the bike saddle I went, and I hammered out mile after mile. That day, I averaged 20 mph. But, more importantly, I was having fun and still in the zone. Rounding the 56-mile marker, I began to count down my last fifty-six miles to the bike finish. Florida roads are smooth for the most part; however, some of them are sealed chipped gravel. I never realized they were dangerous until that day. All was well until mile 81. The closest athlete was at least 100 yards away. I was alone on a flat stretch of road. Ahead, I could see a bright yellow penalty tent with a small legion of officials under the canopy keeping watch over the route. As I approached, cycling my pace speed, something went terribly wrong.

Without warning, I went from upright and pedaling to end over end and sliding twenty feet, cheese grating the skin on my left side. It happened so fast, my feet stayed clipped in the pedals, which made me even more helpless. Once the sliding ended, almost instinctively, I jumped to my feet like a deer and performed an injury assessment on my bike and on myself, in that order. Blood flowed from multiple lacerations. The "road rash" bit me like the sting of a viper. My left hip throbbed from the impact. The officials under the tent ran to me like a mother to her son as I stood there, dazed and confused. I could not wrap my head around what had made me crash.

Anger set in as I tried to pick up my bike and roll it to the tent. The forty yards it took to get there allowed me more of a chance to become even more confused. Why, when I'd had such a great start, had I crashed for no reason? I didn't plan for it, I couldn't control it, nor could I explain it. With thirty-one miles still to bike and then the marathon, I was flustered. But right then, I made a choice. *Swanson, man up, dress the wounds and get back on that bike! Forget the blood, forget the pain.*

The course officials confirmed my bike was not fatally injured, and they found six Subway napkins for me to use to stop the bleeding. I figured that if Subway had saved Jared from death by obesity, their napkins could do a pretty good job bandaging my wounds for thirty-one more miles. With napkins wrapped around my hands, others stuck to my shoulder and left knee, I mounted up again.

I convinced myself I wasn't dead, time would heal my body, and I had an Ironman to finish. Exerting every bit as much strength as it had taken me to get to Ironman in the first place, I got back on the course, determined to finish the race. And that's exactly what I did.

There is no question those last thirty-one miles were ten times more difficult than the first eighty-one. But that didn't stop me, and neither should a crash in your life stop you. So many people wake up to find life crashing down around them. Instead of fighting, they stay on the ground, licking their wounds, sometimes for years. You're not dead. Get up! You have to tell yourself, "No excuses!" You can't control when people let you down, businesses fail, or the doctor confirms the diagnosis; what you can control is how you respond to what happens to you. Pull it together, get back on the saddle, and fight to the finish. For me, all I needed was six *Subway napkins* to get back on the road and finish the race.

Iron Theme:
- Setbacks Will Happen.

Action Steps:
- Don't ever let a little crash crush you.
- You may lose a battle, but you can still win the war.
- Do what you have to do to stop the bleeding; then keep moving forward and never stop.

REMIND ME AGAIN WHY I DO THIS

● ● ●

I was in my second year on an undercover drug unit in the north end of Flint. During one of our investigations, we found a snitch who needed our help. But in this world, he would need to help us first. And that's exactly what he did. The snitch introduced us to the suspect. We ordered up an eight ball of cocaine and set the delivery for 8 p.m. That meant anywhere from 8 p.m. to 11 p.m. in "dope dealer time."

The night was crisp, and stars lit the sky like perfectly placed mood lighting. My partner and I sat in a four-door blue Buick LeSabre, keeping watch for the suspect known as "Shaky Owens." The minutes seemed like hours. Although we both tried to pass the time with meaningless small talk, thoughts of what could happen ran through our heads like a network of freight trains. *What if he decides to shoot? What if he tries to rob us? What if more than one shows up, and the odds fall in their favor?* Despite what happens, one thing remains: The cops have to win.

Out of the darkness he came, his every step through the lot purposeful. His hands were discreetly tucked in his black hoodie. He closed in. I sat in the passenger seat as he leaned into my window, so close I could smell his breath. I handed him the marked bills and he unknowingly delivered a clear plastic bag of powdered cocaine to a police officer. The deal was done.

Counter surveillance tracked his every move back to his house. We had enough probable cause to seek a search warrant. The prosecutor authorized us to raid the house, the District Court judge signed the warrant, and we were within hours of making "Shaky Owen's" day a bit more complicated.

Prior to the raid, all participants gathered for a "pre-raid" briefing. On a snow white dry erase board, the team leader drew up the footprint of the home to be breached. Obstacles such as armor guard, dogs, kids, and guns were identified.

The line-up was assigned. "Hoss takes the ram. Axeman has the shield. Magilla, you have the halogen. Hollywood, Face, and Paris, you're the arrest team. Two uniformed officers take the back and two in the front. Should anybody take fire from inside, find cover and treat it like a barricaded gunman. Worst yet, if one of us gets shot, load and go to the ER in a marked unit. If the bad guy gets shot, call for a rig. Any questions?"

Each team member checked their gear and confirmed their weapons were chambered. We filed into the raid van, and the cars lined up like stud horses at the gates of the Kentucky Derby. Once the cavalry was ready, it was time to roll out. This was the moment. The drive to a target house seemed like it took months. Ten thousand thoughts go through your head as each mile passes.

Talking moves to light chatter and ends in silence as the guys start thinking of their roles. What could go bad? How to respond? Thoughts of family and 10,000 other things swirl through our minds. It's at this point that everyone "reminds themselves why we do this."

We do it because that's what warriors do. We stand against evil forces. We stare death and fear in the face and beg it to fight. It's that fear that stirs the soul to fight cancer or take on a bully. It's that fear that has purchased freedom and brought honor to families.

That is why we fight. If you choose not to fight for the things that are precious to you, then who will? Nobody! You need to put on the battle armor and take up your sword every day. When your battle presents itself, if you are not prepared and mentally ready, you are defeated before you even begin. *"Remind me again why I do this?"* Because I have to.

Iron Theme:
- Choose a Cause and Fight for the Right Reasons!

Action Steps:
- Never fear where you are, if you know you're supposed to be there.
- Be courageous.
- Leave your legacy through victory.

FINISH OR DIE TRYING

●●●

There are times in life when we make a commitment to people, events, or goals that require extraordinary effort from us. Whenever you make a commitment like that, you need to tell others what you are doing. This accomplishes two things.

First of all, you are now bound by accountability to those people. Accountability is a massive motivator that carries warriors to victory. Imagine if you committed to your first marathon, and for months you trained, sacrificed, and invested time and money, only to quit during the race. Worse yet, you quit during your training and never make it to the start. Anyone who knew your goal would now question your commitment, also known as your credibility.

The second benefit of sharing your goals is that it challenges those around you. When you tell someone you're going to accomplish a great task, they become inspired. Humans are instinctively competitive. When they see someone getting something they don't have, they want it. I'm not saying that is always a good thing, but when it comes to personal growth, it can be life-changing. To hear later in life that a friend or, better yet, your kid accomplished a goal and credits you as the one who inspired them, is incredible. That's the magic of accountability.

That is why I do triathlons all over the country. It puts fruit on the tree. It tells people, "I can." Accomplishing extraordinary goals in life separates you from the crowd. It programs you to have an automatic finish attitude. There is no other option but to get it done, whatever the task. You are the one who can get things done.

An interview with a member of SEAL Team 6 is a good example of this. Members of this team are those who killed Bin Laden; they are my kind of people! The interviewer asked the Soldier of Fortune what made SEAL Team 6 so elite. His answer? "We are experts at three things. First, we are experts at communications. Secondly, we are experts at combat movement. Lastly, we are experts at being experts." That's honor!

So here lies the challenge, my friend. If you want to win at life, you need to set extraordinary goals. Tell the world around what you set out to do. Then, *finish it or die trying*.

Iron Theme:
- Never, Ever Quit!

Action Steps:
- Pick a goal.
- Date it.
- Train so hard that when you finish you can repeat the same effort in other areas of your life.

I Loved That Lawn Chair

●●●

This had never happened to me in a competition. My feet weighed twenty pounds, and each step took everything I had to pick them up and set them back down on the pavement. I was in the second 13.1-mile loop, right about the eighteenth mile marker. The evening air was getting more humid, and the sun had just dipped below the Gulf Coast.

The last half of the marathon is always the most difficult for me, more so if it's a double loop design. A double loop is set up so that the halfway mark is also the finish, so when you complete the first leg, your turnaround is also where the competitors finish. I can't begin to describe the mind games that play through your head when everything in your body aches and you are forced to round that stupid cone for another 13.1-mile loop while others are faster and have already finished their second lap, and are crossing the finish line.

In the past, I would have been able dismiss the pain in my legs; that day, however, in addition to the pain, I was sick (I had the bubble guts). I had crashed my bike earlier in the day in addition to not taking the right combination of hydration. My stomach was flipping out. It was a terrible feeling. As I continued to run, for the first time in my competitive career, I came to the place in my head when not only did I need to stop for a minute, but I needed to sit down.

I knew my time was sure to suffer, but I needed rest *now*. My eyes scanned ahead, seeking relief. To my right and up a few hundred feet were the silhouettes of two male spectators. What caught my eye, though, was the unoccupied mesh-style green lawn chair directly behind them. My eyes locked on the chair, and I quickly changed course and staggered over to where they were standing. In total desperation, I managed to stay polite as I asked, "Sir, may I please sit down in your green lawn chair?"

Without hesitation, they both answered in stereo, "Of course."

I turned and sat. They watched to see what was going to happen next, or maybe to make sure I wasn't going to die in their favorite chair. I leaned back, my neck hyperextended and my eyes fixed on the stars. For that short moment, the pain was gone and my stomach was calm. The relief was so overwhelming, I instantly fell asleep right there in that chair. I was exhausted! The minutes seemed like hours as my eyes remained closed. For some reason, though, I could still hear the two spectators talk about my obvious physical condition. They debated back and forth about whether or not they should call for help. All I could do was listen.

What I heard that night was both inspiring and life-changing. "He looks bad. Do you think we should call somebody for him?" the one said.

"No way!" his friend responded. "If he is going to be an Ironman, he'll get up and finish. Let him be."

His words pierced my heart. Like Hulk Hogan from the early days of WrestleMania, my internal batteries started to fire. I forced my head forward, my feet to the ground, and my body up and out of the comfort and security of that green lawn chair. I stood tall and looked both men in the eye as I thanked them with all sincerity. As I stumbled back on the course, I stopped and turned to the guys and said, "I am an Ironman, and I will to finish this!" Two hours later, I finished the remaining 12.2 miles, and I have never seen those men since then.

That night taught me two valuable lessons. First, there are times when you go, go, go and just need to stop for a second and take a break. I learned that it doesn't mean you've quit; it means you're smart enough to put yourself in the position not to quit. If your life seems to be kicking your tail, force yourself to take a technological detox and "chillax." Find a quiet place to sit down alone and kick back. You will be shocked at how therapeutic a short break can be. Taking a break can recharge you and is critical to long-term success.

As an example, while writing this book, I would head outside every evening and sit under the bright moonlight. I'd close my eyes and listen to each sound of the night. I would try to count how many different sounds I could hear from crickets to frogs, vehicles, the rustling of trees, and so on. I loved it and so will you. You deserve it. You need it.

Secondly, when you see someone who is running for a goal, fighting an addiction, finishing a degree, or whatever goal they are struggling to accomplish, and they stumble or get off the path, don't give up on them. Believe in them. Encourage them. Push them. Inspire them. When I heard the words, *"If he is going to be an Ironman, he'll get up,"* that was all the fuel I needed to flip the switch and keep moving forward.

I fear what would have happened if I had taken the advice of guy number one and given up. I would have taken the easy way out. I would have been a quitter. Worse yet, I would have failed myself. That's not what Ironmen are made of; that's not what champions are made of. And that's not what you are made of.

That night, I learned just how much *I loved that green lawn chair.*

Iron Theme:
- Sometimes You Need to Take a Break.

Action Steps:
- Ask yourself if you are getting burned out in an area of your life.
- Take a break and do something completely different, but put a time limit on it.
- Once the break is over, get back to work and finish.

MY SECRET FORMULA REVEALED

● ● ●

One of the most feared enemies in life is ourselves. I found this out over my years as a non-athletic adult. I was apathetic and unmotivated to ever enter the ring of athletics again. I mentioned that in the past, I had been cut from the ninth grade baseball team. That failure sent me into a tailspin of self-doubt that lasted for almost 20 years. Bodybuilding and Ironman healed my wounds. They restored belief in myself and allowed me to recapture the power of competing. Never forget that we are all competitive by nature, and when we don't feed that hunger, we start to lose the edge.

In preparing for both the shows and the triathlons, I used a formula that never failed me. Whenever I felt in the zone, it was because I was using this formula. Conversely, whenever I fell into a slump, it was because I had drifted away.

This strategy can work for anything you want to accomplish in life, a trip of a lifetime, paying off your house, competing in a marathon, or any other worthwhile goal.

1) *Dream*—You need to dream your goal into reality. Ask yourself how your life would be altered forever if you finished what you set out to do. What would your kids or your friends think once you completed what you had set out to do? How would you view yourself, knowing that you had accomplished your goal? When Ironman first ran in 1978, its motto was coined then and remains today: *"Swim 2.4 miles. Bike 112. Run 26.2 and brag for the rest of your life."*

2) *Visualize*—You need to see it, feel it, taste it, and hear it before you achieve it. I remember closing my eyes and watching and listening to the ocean water crash against the shoreline. I could feel the soft, white sand between my toes. I saw myself crossing the finish line, and as I did, the announcer told me that I was an Ironman. I was there before I was even there. Once you visualize what you set out to do and have created the mental picture, it is no longer a dream. It's almost a reality, and now all you have to do is go through the motions. Visualization is a massive tool you need to use to achieve your greatness.

3) *Have Passion*—Most think of passion as physical intimacy, which is not all bad. Wouldn't you agree that the more "passion" enters into a physical relationship, the better the feeling? Of course! That applies to your success as well. When you set out to grab hold of a dream, you must do so with passion. When you talk about it, people should see your energy and feel your excitement. Your body language should change, and your audience should leave knowing there is no way you won't finish what you set out to do. The more passion you have to make it happen, the greater the odds will be in your favor.

4)   *Be 100%* Committed—There can be no halfway effort. You need to be "sold out" to what you set out to do. There can be no honeymoon phase. Every day, until it's done, is a workday. Think back to all the false promises you've made to yourself or others. The more you do, the more those around you will see you as "all talk." You must be consumed by your goal. You must stick to the plan every day. Take with you the good and the bad days and never stop! Imagine if you only developed as a baby 99% of the way, or if the manufacturer only put 99% of the parts in your engine. What would it be like if a bridge was only 99% completed? Either go all the way or don't even leave the garage.

5)   *Surround Yourself with Like-minded People*— The fact remains that anytime you try to better yourself or do something that others only wish they could do, there will be critics. More people want us to fail than succeed. Sad, but true. Knowing this, I use that criticism as jet fuel. If someone tells me I can't do it, *watch me.* I found that during my training, the more I worked out with former champions, the more I felt like a champion. Like-minded folks have already gotten the crown and want you to have it as well. They will keep you encouraged and focused. If they are a true leader, they will do anything in their power to help you achieve your dreams as well. That's the power of like-minded people. Be cautious of those who hate— don't hang with them. Don't seek their advice or ask their opinion, unless, of course, you really want to hear it. Like-minded champions build; critics tear down. If you want to seek riches, meet with wealthy people. If you want to be an incredible musician, work with the first chair. You want to

own a mall, talk to a real estate tycoon. Stay with the like-minded.

This is my secret formula revealed! I continue to use it and find it to be so powerful. Try it.

Iron Theme:
- Follow This Plan to Succeed!

Action Steps:
- Dream.
- Visualize.
- Have passion.
- Be 100% committed.
- Be with like-minded people who encourage you.

LIVE ON THE EDGE

"If You're Not Living on the Edge, You're Taking Up Too Much Space!"

— Marcus Luttrell, author of *Lone Survivor*

●●●

The journey from *Tinman to IRONMAN* demands everything you've got. And on that list better be *risk*. I've done some crazy things in my life. I graduated with a master's degree from the University of Michigan. I'm a police officer and a paramedic; a medical examiner and investigator; I've started businesses and sold businesses; bought, sold, and developed real estate, and of course, finished multiple Ironman events, among so many other adventures. Each time I do something big, it comes with the possibility to succeed or fail, but I know that going into it.

When an idea comes into my head, I immediately start to evaluate the *risk* factor. I consider the pros and the cons. I use the power of discernment. Discernment is the ability to look at what it's going to take to make the idea work. *Do I have the necessary resources? Can I afford it? Is there a market? Is there time?*

I describe discernment like peeling an onion. With each layer removed, you get deeper into the core and closer to your answer. It's during this process that you need to be honest with yourself about your ability. Be realistic and use common sense; the bigger the decision, the more you'd better use good discernment.

Once you have evaluated your idea and feel it's viable, then it's time to use discipline. Discipline is the "stick to it" stuff. It's what you do when everything in your body says, "No" and you have to convince your heart to say, "Go." That's discipline. When it comes to Ironman training, bodybuilding, or a strict diet, mental preparation and competing are difficult. During the process, I remind myself that living on the edge is lonely, but I wouldn't want it any other way.

Ninety percent of those you pass on the street don't think that way. Most people in life are what my buddy TW calls, "Tire Kickers." They go through life always dreaming about doing something, buying something, or starting something, and never take the *risk* and do it. They kick the tire their whole life. Those people don't want to put forth the effort and use good discernment. They would never have the discipline to see their idea through to the end. But what if your idea was a great idea? What if what you wanted to do would work if you only had a plan? Dave Ramsey tells us that, "The only difference between a dream and a goal is the plan." You need to live on the edge. Make the plan and try things. Some may fail and some will work. But if you never try, you will never know.

I love starting something from nothing. My wife asks me every time I register for another Ironman, "Why do you want to do another one?"

My answer, "Because I can!" I don't say it in a condescending or disrespectful way, but as long as the Lord gives me the physical ability to compete, I will. Ironman forces me to be disciplined. The discipline I practice benefits me in everything I do.

My plea to you is to identify in your life those things that you have always wanted to do and make a plan to do them. Take the risk. So what if you fail? At least you will have the right to tell the world you failed courageously. If you want to see an example of ultimate courage, check out www.lonesurvivor.com. There you will find the story of Navy SEAL Marcus Luttrell, and understand why, *"If you're not living on the edge, you're taking up too much space."*

Iron Theme:
- Take Risks!

Action Steps:
- Evaluate the pros and cons. This is called discernment.
- Determine if you are truly capable of achieving your desired result.
- Be disciplined every day.

HERE TODAY, GONE TOMORROW

●●●

I went to bed on a cold, dark, February night with my phone on the nightstand to my left, ready for a call. Like hundreds of nights before, I was the on-call Medical Examiner Investigator. As the moon lit the sky around 1 a.m., the phone startled me from a deep sleep. It was my dispatcher.

"Hey sir, I have a nasty one for you," he said.

Still trying to gain my senses, I told him I needed two minutes to get my head together, and I would call right back. That was vitally important since I could tell whatever I was about to hear was not going to be pretty. And I was right. About two minutes later, I made good on my promise and called back. "What's up?" I asked.

"Sir, there was a fire in the north end, and four babies died. They're already at Hurley ER, and sir, I've been told they're pretty bad and need to be identified." POW! It hit me like a ton of bricks.

How the heck do four little kids die at once? I thought to myself. I told my dispatcher I would be on my way, hung up the phone, and prayed, "Lord, strengthen my heart, give me wisdom, and allow me the courage to deal with whatever I must deal with." I got dressed, hurried to my car, and started the fifteen-minute drive to the scene of the nightmare. As I pulled into the ER, I continued my mental preparation. In this field, that's critical; otherwise, people get hurt. The thought of those four little babies suffering at the hands of a raging fire, the smoke taking their air hostage, weighed heavy on my heart.

I parked my truck in hospital parking, gathered my gear, and walked to the morgue. The closer I got, the more intense the radio traffic from those still at the fire became. My first contact was with both hospital security and the ambulance crew from the scene. I could see they were emotionally taxed. "Hey guys, can anyone tell me what happened?" I inquired.

One of the EMT's hung his head, then spoke. "One of the kids' uncles was watching them and left to go to the store. He came back to the apartment and then somehow, the kitchen caught on fire, and he jumped out the window," the EMT intoned. "Inside were left a one, two, three, and four-year-old."

I found out later he passed out on the couch while he was cooking something on the stove, and the kitchen went up in flames. The kids were trapped upstairs.

Although she was succinct, I didn't need any more details. We left the lot and were escorted into the morgue where the victims were held. I went into professional mode and prepared to do what I had been called to do—examine, identify, and document the victims.

Striding through the main door, down the hall, and into the storage cooler, I stared in disbelief at four white body bags that held within them the remains of the silent victims, all under the age of five. In order to protect the integrity of the Medical Examiner's investigation, I cannot disclose what I saw, smelled, or felt. What I can say is that, on that night, I saw more death from one scene than on any other day of my career. It wasn't at all what I had imagined it would be. It was worse.

After spending nearly three hours in the morgue, my part was done. The memory of that night will never leave me. Burnt flesh is one of the most grotesque stenches outside of decomposition you will ever smell.

Why do things like that happen in our society? Why do tragedy and devastation strip young people of their lives? There are just some things to which we will never know the answers. But when those things happen, the best response is to reflect on life. We need to take inventory of what we have and who we love. Many times, our worst day is a thousand times better than the best day of the majority of the world's population. We'd better treasure the precious people in our lives because they can be taken away in a vapor.

At night, I go to my kids' rooms after they are asleep and kiss their tender foreheads. I feel the warmth of their breath on my cheek. I pray over them and beg for protection and safety and thank God that He has entrusted them to my care. My plea is that, as you hear this, you will forget about the dumb stuff in life that takes time and energy away from those things that mean the most. Go to the people you love and tell them you love them. Show them you love them and live like you love them.

Do it today because one thing life guarantees is that everything is *here today and gone tomorrow,* including you!

Iron Theme:
- You Will Die Someday.

Action Steps:
- Appreciate those in your life you could not live without.
- Tell these people that you love them and show them how much.
- Live like you will never die, but know your book of life will one day close. What will your book include?

26.2

(THE MOST IMPORTANT CHAPTER OF THIS BOOK)

● ● ●

Over the last twenty-five chapters, you have read stories of a *Tinman* who gave everything he had and transformed his life to become an *IRONMAN*. This was my story. What's your story? What road are you on? Are you satisfied with your life as it is right now, or do you want more? Have your hopes and dreams been buried under the dust of a critic's negativity? Or have you let yourself down?

Not anymore!

I want you to make a decision right now to take action. Write down what you want in your life. Be specific and set a date to get it done. Do everything in your power to get done what you need to do. Most importantly, once you achieve it, repeat the process it took to get it done. That's what takes you from a *Tinman to an IRONMAN*!

Start Today!

Iron Themes Reviewed

1) Believe in Second Chances.
2) Every Choice Has a Consequence.
3) Stay Focused.
4) Be You!
5) Turn Defeat into Victory!
6) Take Pride in Your Body.
7) Have Willpower.
8) No Excuses; Make Changes.
9) Prepare and Train.
10) Be Tuned in to Others.
11) Beat Adversity!
12) Turn Fear into Focus.
13) Don't Sweat the Small Stuff.
14) Don't Jump to Conclusions.
15) Never Cheat!
16) Check Your Pride.
17) Stress Can Be a Friend.
18) Inspiration Drives Motivation!
19) Setbacks Will Happen.
20) Choose a Cause and Fight for Right Reasons!
21) Never, Ever Quit!
22) Sometimes You Need to Take a Break.
23) Follow This Plan to Succeed.
24) Take Risks!
25) You Will Die Someday.
26) Start Today!

ABOUT THE AUTHOR

Chris Swanson has been a police officer for over twenty years. He is the Undersheriff for the Office of Sheriff, Genesee County, Michigan, and commands 239 sworn personnel in one of America's most dangerous communities, Flint, Michigan. He has a master's degree from the University of Michigan, where he has also served on the faculty since 1997. A three-time *Ironman* finisher and amateur natural body builder, Chris Swanson inspires and motivates at public high schools, churches, businesses, and police departments throughout the United States. His teachings on the laws of leadership, personal growth, and how success changes lives are loaded with practical application. The enthusiasm of Chris Swanson is both entertaining and infectious.

Visit him on Facebook or his website at www.swansonleadership.com.